T0327848

PROPAGANDOPOLIS

A Century of Propaganda from Around the World

BRADLEY DAVIES

FUEL

ROBERT PECKHAM
Fear, Truth and the Spectacular History of Propaganda

The images in this anthology, selected from the Propagandopolis online collection, are organised from A to Z by country – Afghanistan to Zimbabwe – and range from the early twentieth century to the 2000s. Although the principal medium reproduced here is the poster, the book also includes a miscellany of street murals, billboards, brochures, booklets, magazine covers, and film stills. Wrenched from the continuum of the internet and oddly juxtaposed within an encyclopaedic format, the images – variously naïve, avant-garde, totalitarian, modernist, and contemporary – invite us to reflect on propaganda's meanings and purposes, its history and future. Can political art be good if the cause it was designed to propagandise is bad? What happens when the medium survives the message?

In his rambling, rabidly antisemitic manifesto *Mein Kampf*, published in 1925, Adolf Hitler had a lot to say about the art of propaganda. 'Ever since I have been scrutinizing political events,' he wrote, 'I have taken a tremendous interest in propagandist activity.' For him, the First World War was a turning point since it revealed the importance of 'understanding the emotional ideas of the great masses', and finding an appropriate psychological form to move them. Propaganda was a means of advancing a cause by tapping into and manipulating deep-seated predispositions and prejudices. 'The receptivity of the masses is very limited, their intelligence is small,' Hitler declared, 'but their power of forgetting is enormous. In consequence of these facts, all effective propaganda must be limited to a very few points and must harp on these in slogans until the last member of the public understands what you want him to understand by your slogan.'[1]

Less than a decade later, Hitler had transmogrified into the *Führer* and set up the Ministry of Public Enlightenment and Propaganda under Joseph Goebbels who now had oversight of the press, books, art, theatre, music, films, and radio. Propaganda was key to the Nazi 'coordination' (*Gleichschaltung*) of German society. Its secret, Goebbels claimed, was 'to permeate the person it aims to grasp, without his even noticing that he is being permeated'.[2]

Leni Riefenstahl's *Triumph of the Will*, which was personally commissioned by Hitler to celebrate the 1934 Nazi rally at Nuremberg, ranks as perhaps 'the most purely propagandistic film ever made'.[3] This is propaganda art that plays on hope and desire, at the same time as it summons fear as the underside of exultation. The synchronised motion of the marching troops doesn't just warn of violence to come, it reaffirms the ideal of the sublimated citizen and asks us to imagine what would happen if the coordinated parade broke down. Without the Party and its paternalistic credo – without propaganda – the unified mass would shatter into chaos.

Triumph of the Will. Publicity press-book cover for the 1935 film directed by Leni Riefenstahl.

The word 'propaganda', from the Latin *propagare* to propagate, to spread, originated during the seventeenth-century Counter Reformation as the Catholic Church fought to stem the tide of heresy by promoting the true faith through the establishment of the *Sacra congregatio de propaganda fide* (the Sacred Congregation for the Propagation of the Faith) to direct missionary activity, and later through the Pontifical Urban College of Propaganda (named after Pope Urban VIII). The opening scene of Riefenstahl's film highlights this devotional provenance as the camera dwells on the cross-shaped shadow of the plane that bears the *Führer* messiah-like through billowing clouds, and later tracks across ecstatic crowds. The message from on high to this enraptured congregation echoes the injunction in Genesis to 'Go forth and multiply, and fill the earth and subdue it.'

There is nothing new about the deployment of visual art to further political and religious causes. Although it may be anachronistic to speak of early modern 'propaganda', we can nonetheless trace new forms of public communication back to the advent of Gutenberg's movable-type printing press in the mid fifteenth century. Martin Luther proved to be a master of this new medium, disseminating his radical dogma via inexpensive pamphlets (*Flugschriften*, or 'flying writings') that combined accessible text with striking woodcut illustrations. At the same time, rulers sought to consolidate and deepen their grip on power by commissioning glorifying images of themselves in the form of medallions, statues and paintings.

By the end of the eighteenth century, more recognisably modern forms of propaganda had arisen. During the French Revolution, caricatures, engravings, songs, slogans, and clothing – the display tricolour of cockades (knots of ribbons), for example, and the wearing of cotton pantaloons in place of posh breeches – were being used to inculcate revolutionary fervour in citizens.[4] In part because of the terror with which the Revolution came to be associated, however, propaganda acquired negative connotations. Its meaning shifted to include the circulation of biased and misleading information. Industrialisation, the rise of a mass consumer society and the advent of commercial branding were all key to the development of propaganda in the late nineteenth and early twentieth centuries. The promotion of political interests began to overlap with the marketing of products and services. Health messages and political slogans converged with commercial logos and ad copy.

The First World War further highlighted the importance of propaganda. As the American political scientist Harold Lasswell observed in 1927, 'The history of the late War shows that modern war must be fought on three fronts: the military front, the economic front, and the propaganda front.'[5] In 1917, President Wilson had set up a Committee on Public Information (CPI) with a remit to influence public opinion in support of the war through the distribution of pamphlets, posters, radio broadcasts, films, and public talks. The journalist George Creel was put in charge, and while he argued that patriotic messaging was vital for the survival of American democracy, the word 'propaganda' was to be avoided, since it had sinister overtones. The creation of the CPI, Creel acknowledged, was 'a plain publicity proposition, a vast enterprise in salesmanship, the world's greatest adventures in advertising'.[6]

Authoritarian states invariably loom large in *Propagandopolis* since propaganda is closely associated with totalitarianism: fascist Italy, Nazi Germany, the Soviet Union, communist China, and North Korea. 'History stopped in 1936,' George Orwell once observed, the year that Stalin launched the Great Purge, and the Spanish Civil War began. 'Early in life I had noticed that no event is ever correctly reported in a newspaper,' Orwell wrote, 'but in Spain, for the first time, I saw newspaper reports which did not bear any relation to the facts, not even the relationship which is implied in an ordinary lie.' History was no long being written 'in terms of what happened but of what ought to have happened according to various "party lines"'.[7]

The A-to-Z structure of this book, however, reminds us that propaganda isn't just tethered to totalitarianism; it has far more complex colonial, post-colonial and democratic histories. In developing their propaganda, Nazis borrowed from the burgeoning field of American public relations. Like PR executives, they set out to sell things to the masses, manipulating behaviour for profit. Among the books that influenced Goebbels was *Crystallizing Public Opinion* (1923) by the Viennese-born, American PR pioneer Edward Bernays.[8]

Bernays, who was Sigmund Freud's nephew, drew upon psychoanalytic theories to explain the novel techniques being harnessed to manage the masses. Propaganda, he argued, was a modern instrument to 'fight for productive ends and help bring order out of chaos'. 'The conscious and intelligent manipulation of the organized habits and opinions of the masses is an important element in democratic society,' he wrote in *Propaganda* (1928). 'Those who manipulate this unseen mechanism of society constitute an invisible government which is the true ruling power of our country.'[9]

Opponents of this propaganda pointed to its insidious and profit-hungry nature, and to the corrupting complicity between media and corporate interests. Free speech was being eroded and citizens were losing their independence. Pervasive propaganda was impeding critical thinking and ultimately undermining democratic processes. 'Control of opinion is the greatest weapon of anti-social forces,' the philosopher and educator John Dewey noted in 1931. 'We are ruled by headlines, publicity agents and "counsellors of public relations." Propaganda can be attacked, and its force weakened only by one agency – informed publicity.'[10] A few years later an Institute of Propaganda Analysis was set up to teach Americans how to recognise and challenge propaganda's psychological manipulations.

Other propaganda critics noted how a capitalist 'culture industry' had emerged, relying upon the same exploitative psycho-techniques 'to overpower the customer, who is conceived as absent-minded or resistant'.[11] This understanding would later be developed by the French philosopher Guy Debord to argue that in a mass-media, image-saturated world, driven by commercial imperatives, new propagandistic procedures had turned people into passive consumers.[12]

By the late 1980s, free market economics and industrial deregulation were being widely championed. It was against this backdrop that Noam Chomsky and his colleague Edward Herman proposed a 'propaganda model' for studying the different 'distorting filters' that worked to skew the media. 'The mass media serve as a system for communicating messages and symbols to the general populace,' they wrote. 'It is their function to amuse, entertain, and inform, and to inculcate individuals with the values, beliefs, and codes of behavior that will integrate them into the institutional structures of the larger society. In a world of concentrated wealth and major conflicts of class interest, to fulfill this role requires systematic propaganda.'[13] The meaning of democracy had been subverted, they argued; it no longer connoted an open society in which people were active participants in political life, but rather a society in which information was 'kept narrowly and rigidly controlled' by a self-interested media. 'Propaganda is to a democracy what the bludgeon is to a totalitarian state,' Chomsky reflected gloomily in 1991, the year that the Soviet Union collapsed.[14]

Meanwhile, from the mid-twentieth century, art was explicitly probing the propagandistic features of mass-media culture. In Jasper Johns's *White Flag*, completed in 1955, newsprint is just visible beneath the painting's elegant, waxy finish suggesting that patriotism is undergirded by the invisible influence of a propagandising press. The propagandistic mechanisms driving consumerism became central to pop art from the 1960s, including Andy Warhol's images of Mao, Nixon, and Campbell's soup, and Roy Lichtenstein's appropriated comic strips, and later Barbara Kruger's anti-consumer slogan pasteups.

As an anthology, *Propagandopolis* reminds us that much artmaking exists in an ambiguous space between propaganda and commerce. Historically, artists have earned their keep with commissions, painting religious themes and portraits for their wealthy patrons. While the art produced in communist and other totalitarian states tends to be viewed as suspect because of its political biases, contemporary art largely acquires its value by differentiating itself both from the brazenly political and the overtly commercial.

In this sense, it is the ultimate propaganda, making the case for its own exceptionalism by suggesting that true art is art with no extraneous case to make.[15]

Often the most committed and adept propagandists are those who give the loudest warnings about propaganda's truth-crushing propensities and its sinister collusion with fear. 'There's only one solution to propaganda. Telling the truth without fear,' the political commentator Tucker Carlson proclaimed in a 2023 post on X to promote his new streaming platform, TCN. Today, however, the word 'propaganda' has a whiff of the antediluvian. Information is no longer analogue and centrally coordinated but digital and radically diffused, moving across the globe in real time. Debate now centres on misinformation, disinformation and 'fake news', rather than propaganda. Fears coalesce around AI, hacking and the manipulation of public opinion via memes on social media, as well as the use of bots to fabricate an illusionary consensus and virality. Was Bernays wrong, then, when he claimed that propaganda would never die? Does new technology herald propaganda's obsolescence, or perhaps its absolute distillation and ubiquity?

1 Adolf Hitler, *Mein Kampf*, trans. Ralph Manheim (Boston: Houghton Mifflin, 1943), 176, 180–181.

2 Richard J. Evans, *The Third Reich in Power* (New York: Penguin, 2005), 127.

3 Susan Sontag, 'Fascinating Fascism', *New York Review of Books* (6 February 1975).

4 An exhibition at the Fashion and Textile Museum in London, curated by the design historian Amber Butchart, explored the propagandistic use of fabrics in furnishing and fashion; *The Fabric of Democracy: Propaganda Textiles from the French Revolution to Brexit* (September 2023–March 2024).

5 Harold D. Lasswell, *Propaganda Technique in World War I* (New York: Peter Smith, [1927] 1938), 214.

6 George Creel, *How We Advertised America* (New York and London: Harper & Brothers, 1920), 4.

7 George Orwell, 'Looking Back on the Spanish War' [1943]. In: *A Collection of Essays* (San Diego: Harcourt Brace Jovanovich, 1953), 188-209 (197).

8 Edward L. Bernays, *Biography of an Idea: Memoirs of Public Relations Counsel Edward L. Bernays* (New York, Simon and Schuster, 1965), 652.

9 Edward L. Bernays, *Propaganda* (New York: Liveright Publishing, 1936), 159, 9.

10 John Dewey, *The Later Works, 1925–1953. Volume 6: 1931–1932*, ed. Jo An Boydston (Carbondale, IL: Southern Illinois University Press, 2008), 178.

11 Theodor W. Adorno and Max Horkheimer, 'The Culture Industry: Enlightenment as Mass Deception.' In: *Dialectic of Enlightenment: Philosophical Fragments*, ed. Gunzelin Schmid Noerr and trans. Edmund Jephcott (Stanford, CA: University of Stanford Press, 2002), 94–136 (133).

12 Guy Debord, *The Society of the Spectacle*, trans. Donald Nicholson Smith (Cambridge, MA: MIT Press, 1994).

13 Edward Herman and Noam Chomsky, *Manufacturing Consent: The Political Economy of the Mass Media* (New York: Pantheon Books, 1988), 1.

14 Noam Chomsky, *Media Control: The Spectacular Achievements of Propaganda* (New York: Seven Stories Press, [1991] 2002), 20–21.

15 Boris Groys, *Art Power* (Cambridge, MA: MIT Press, 2013), 4–9.

CONTENTS

On the bottle: **Vodka**. Behind the figure: **Babrak**. A leaflet produced in the 1980s showing Babrak Karmal, the President of communist Afghanistan, hugging a bottle of hammer-and-sickle-branded vodka. Propaganda produced by the mujahideen throughout the war often depicted the Soviet-backed government as being un-Islamic.

The journey of death. An anti-Soviet poster from 1980 calling for a boycott of the Olympic Games (due to take place in Moscow that year) in protest at the Soviet invasion of Afghanistan. It is a parody of a tourist travel poster, showing a bayonet impaling Misha, the Olympic mascot, with the text at the bottom reading 'Aeroflot' (the famous Soviet airline).

Allahu Akbar [God is the greatest]. An anti-Soviet poster from the Afghan-Soviet War (1979–1989). The exact date of this poster is unknown (a number of secondary sources state 1986). The publisher and provenance are also uncertain, with some sources stating it was drawn by a British artist.

The transformation of an individual's personality while using illegal drugs. Passers-by stop to look at an anti-drug poster, Kabul, Afghanistan, 2004. The design shows a man smoking drugs while shadowy, skeletal Death lurks behind him. The poster was one of many produced by the United Nations and other international organisations as part of a years-long anti-drug campaign in Afghanistan following the country's invasion by coalition forces in 2001.

Jungle guerrilla, present yourself with your gun – you will be rewarded, you will be treated well. A Portuguese leaflet (c.1970) from the Colonial War (1961–1974), urging guerrillas then fighting in Angola, Guinea and Mozambique to surrender themselves and their weapons to the military.

A Cuban illustration for a 1995 cover of *Tricontinental*, a magazine published by the Organization of Solidarity with the People of Asia, Africa and Latin America (OSPAAAL) – a political movement founded in 1966 during the Tricontinental Conference in Havana. OSPAAAL quickly became Cuba's primary propaganda outlet, generating posters celebrating Marxist movements around the world. Often featuring brightly coloured and tonally simplified depictions of guerrilla fighters, the posters were usually reproduced in several languages. When this issue appeared, Angola was approaching the end of what would be a 26-year civil war. Cuba had sent tens of thousands of troops in support of the People's Movement for the Liberation of Angola (MPLA) against the anti-communist National Union for the Total Independence of Angola (UNITA).

Text above the bottle: **Against all illnesses**. Text at the bottom: **Murky water prepared by 'hekims'** [healers] **will send you to hospital**. Issued in Moscow in 1960 by the Institute of Health Education, this Soviet Armenian poster warns against folk healers peddling supposed cures and elixirs. The centralised health system of the USSR was built on scientific principles, and traditional medicines (alongside religions) were banned.

The twentieth century – Be embraced, you millions! A cover from the Austrian magazine *Die Muskete* (1916), showing the machine of war smothering the masses. The artwork is by Fritz Gareis, a prominent illustrator of political publications in Vienna at the time. The line 'Be embraced, you millions' is from 'Ode to Joy' (1785) by Friedrich Schiller. From the very beginning of the First World War, *Die Muskete* had agreed to follow a 'patriotic line', only reproducing material condemning enemy nations. However, as the war progressed, the magazine became increasingly critical of the war in general, often illustrating its covers with striking anti-war imagery.

Vienna 1938, the Urania observatory displays a giant poster of Hitler's face and the word **JA** (YES), urging Austrians to vote in favour of the German annexation of Austria in the upcoming plebiscite. The idea of a unified Germany and Austria had existed for several decades, but the movement for the Anschluss ('joining') only gained real momentum in the 1930s after the Nazi Party had won power in Germany. Initially the Austrian Chancellor Kurt von Schuschnigg had resisted Nazi demands in this direction, but with mounting internal and external pressure, he was eventually forced to acquiesce. On 12 March German forces crossed the border into Austria unopposed, annexing the country the following day. After suppressing all potential opposition, the April plebiscite confirmed widespread support for the action, with an apparent 99.7 per cent of respondents voting in favour of Anchluss.

Villain! Behold your work! The figure of Death shows Kaiser Wilhelm II a mass grave of his making. This illustration by Gisbert Combaz (1869–1941) is from the First World War (1916). A Belgian lawyer, writer and versatile artist, Combaz worked variously as a painter, poster designer and sculptor, among other professions. He made a series of anti-German illustrations that were published in newspapers, as well as being reproduced on posters and postcards throughout the war, this one being the most famous.

This 1937 front cover of the Brazilian magazine *Anauê!* shows Santa Claus donning his red jacket over a green Integralist uniform. Emerging as a nationalist movement in the 1930s, the Integralists were inspired by (though distinct from) European fascism. Green was their colour and 'Anauê!' (supposedly an indigenous Tupi word meaning 'you are my brother!') was their greeting. Some Integralists opposed Santa Claus as being insufficiently Brazilian, instead promoting a native, forest-dwelling, grandpa figure called 'Vovô Índio' who, like Santa, brought gifts for good children and spurned the bad. The newspaper *Correio da Manhã* embraced Vovô Índio's ascent to the 'pedestal formerly occupied by a foreign puppet'. Ultimately Vovô Índio gained little traction and his popularity dwindled towards the end of the decade.

The cover of *Democracy and Communism* (1961), an anti-communist publication, produced by the General Staff of the Brazilian Army. The book comprises a collection of articles – many previously published in the magazine *National Defence* – detailing the methods and apparent threats posed by communists. These include contributions with titles such as: 'How to Beat Communism', 'Freedom and Communism', 'What is Communism?', 'Communist Propaganda', 'How the Communist Party Works' and 'How Communists Seize Power and Keep It'. In 1964, prompted by fears of communism, the Brazilian Army overthrew the government of João Goulart in a coup that ushered in over two decades of military rule.

An anti-free trade poster showing Death marching on a factory, carrying a scythe labelled 'Free Trade'. This British poster was published in 1909 by the Budget Protest League, an organisation established in the same year, in opposition to the so-called People's Budget of the Liberal Chancellor, David Lloyd George. The League produced thousands of posters condemning the People's Budget as a socialist initiative (as it aimed to introduce higher taxes to fund welfare programmes) while also strenuously condemning free trade, a policy that both the League and the Conservative Party decried as the source of British industrial decline.

This preparatory sketch for a poster dates from the Second World War (c.1943) and shows a swastika being crushed between the jaws of a Russia–Britain trap, with text below reading 'Fascism Shall Perish'. The poster seems never to have been issued, but it was likely conceived as part of the British 'Unity of Strength' series that celebrated the country's wartime alliances, especially with the Soviet Union.

An illustration by Leslie Illingworth for *Punch* magazine. Dating from the start of the Second World War (6 November 1939) it is titled 'The Combat' and shows a lone aircraft labelled 'Freedom' flying over a European city towards a colossal Nazi monster. Both British and French roundels appear on the aircraft's wings, and the pilot is haloed.

VICTORY IS VITAL!

GERMANS WOULD ROB WEST AFRICANS OF THEIR PRODUCE

The front cover of a British anti-German propaganda pamphlet from the Second World War (c.1940) intended for distribution in West Africa. The illustrations show German soldiers abusing locals, while the text warns the reader of the cruelty and greed of the Germans in contrast to the purported fairness of the British.

For King and Country. A British propaganda poster from the Second World War published and distributed during the prelude to the Battle of Singapore in 1942, where the British lost to the Japanese. Churchill called the fall of Singapore 'the worst disaster and largest capitulation in British history'.

The famous British election poster used by the Labour Party in the run up to the 1945 general election. Clement Attlee served as Prime Minister for the next six years after winning a surprise landslide victory.

A poster published by the Liberal Party as part of their 'Liberal Europe Campaign' during the 1975 referendum on continued membership of the European Communities (EC). A symbolic family stand in a doorway opened onto a bright picture of Europe, with text below listing some purported benefits of staying in the EC for each family member. Ultimately voters opted to remain, with 67 per cent voting in favour.

FLIES AND DISEASE.

**KILL THE FLY
and
SAVE THE CHILD.**

A public health illustration (1910) published in *The Medical Officer*, a journal printed in London from 1897 until 1973. It was one of many illustrations and posters issued around the time alerting citizens – especially mothers – to the dangers of flies. This information would eventually make its way into official government propaganda, especially during the World Wars. *The Medical Officer* also offered broader public health advice on topics such as tuberculosis prevention, food and personal hygiene, dental health, sanitation and more.

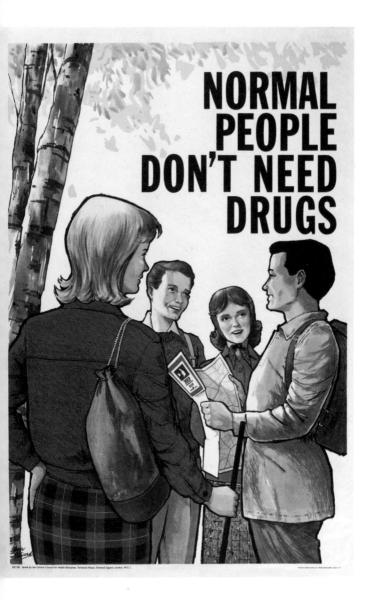

This anti-drug poster (c.1965) was part of a campaign launched by the Central Council for Health Education. The council was composed of ministers, MPs, doctors and other medical professionals, and initiated a number of public health campaigns throughout the 1950s and 1960s.

May 9 – Victory Day. A poster showing a dynamic image of a hand holding a PPSh-41 submachine gun. It was designed in 1980 by Racho Burov for Victory Day which, alongside many other Eastern Bloc countries, was celebrated by the communist People's Republic of Bulgaria on 9 May. (The German Instrument of Surrender was signed on 8 May 1945 at 22:43 Central European time, or 9 May 1945, at 00:43 Moscow time.)

A poster from the Second World War (1943) warning against careless talk, showing a Goebbels-headed 'rumour' snake hatching from a swastika-speckled egg. Signed 'Hoch' and issued by the Director of Public Information.

Above: **We will win**. An East German poster published in the 1970s showing the head of Salvador Allende against the national flag, with a vast crowd before him. Allende came to power in the 1970 presidential election at the head of the Popular Unity coalition, a group comprising the country's largest leftist parties. He was overthrown in September 1973 after a coup led by General Augusto Pinochet with US support.

Right: **Stop the massacre! Solidarity with Chile!** This poster from the World Federation of Democratic Youth (WFDY) depicts the Chilean leader Augusto Pinochet. It was published shortly after the coup that ousted President Salvador Allende and installed Pinochet in his place.

The coup was launched on 11 September 1973 against the Popular Unity government of Allende, who had been Chilean President for three years, heading a coalition that included most of the country's major leftist parties. The coup was followed by a period of repression against leftists and dissidents that was condemned by foreign organisations such as the WFDY. Chile was ruled by Pinochet's military junta until 1988 when international pressure forced a referendum and he was voted from power.

HALTE AU MASSACRE!
SOLIDARITÉ AVEC LE CHILI!

Publié par la Fédération Mondiale de la Jeunesse Démocratique

Peking, 1958, a man looks at large low-reliefs depicting a rat (its body made of rat-skins) and a fly, both impaled by nails. This mural was produced as part of China's famous 'Four Evils campaign' for the eradication of rats, flies, mosquitoes and sparrows. Blamed for the transmission of disease or, in the case of the sparrows, for eating grain, citizens were urged to kill them wherever they were encountered. However, the drive had unforeseen harmful consequences, in particular the killing of sparrows which led to a sharp rise in locust populations. Partly thanks to the advice of ornithologist Tso-hsin Cheng, who warned of further disastrous ecological outcomes, the 'Smash Sparrows campaign' was halted in 1960, and the Four Evils campaign continued, with bedbugs substituted for sparrows.

除四害！

第一九五六年起，在十二年内，在一切可能的地方，基
本上消灭老鼠，消灭麻雀，消灭苍蝇，消灭蚊子。
在繁殖几年消灭蚊蝇为主，做人人参加除四害

Exterminate the four pests! A 1958 poster from the 'Four Evils campaign', showing a mosquito, fly, sparrow and rat all impaled on a single sword. The government had identified these four species as destructive vermin to be eradicated. The campaign with the precept 'Man must conquer nature' was officially ended in 1961, after its implementation caused severe ecological imbalances which in turn, along with other policies of The Great Leap Forward, contributed to widespread famine.

National Unity (1958), a watercolour by Jin Meisheng (1902–1989), showing the peoples of China marching together, waving various flags and carrying a portrait of Mao. Meisheng was a prominent Chinese artist renowned for his calendar designs. From the 1950s onwards he worked with the Shanghai People's Fine Arts Publishing House, which published most of his work.

敬爱的小平同志——钢铁长城

Beloved comrade Xiaoping – great wall of steel. This 1994 illustration shows a waving Deng Xiaoping (1904–1997) with the People's Liberation Army advancing behind him. Deng was Paramount Leader of China from 1978 to 1989 and this poster was one of a series produced by the Sichuan Fine Arts Publishing House to celebrate his life and power.

Above: This 1974 poster published in Shanghai shows soldiers at a shooting range training to fire from bicycles. Bicycle infantry were deployed to great effect in a number of twentieth-century conflicts. During the Japanese invasion of China in 1937 and the later invasion of British colonies in Southeast Asia, tens of thousands of Japanese troops used bicycles in their rapid advance across the continent (which some later called the 'Bicycle Blitzkrieg'). During the Vietnam War (1955–1975), the North Vietnamese Army and Viet-Cong also used bikes. Their practice of resupplying troops mid-battle was so successful that the US Senate Foreign Relations Committee dedicated a hearing to the issue, during which the journalist Harrison Salisbury offered his analysis: 'I literally believe that without bikes they [the NVA/VC] would have to get out of the war.'

Left: A poster (1964) depicting climbers summiting Mount Everest, carrying with them the national flag, a copy of the Little Red Book and a bust of Mao. Such posters were intended for display in classrooms, to celebrate the 1960 expedition that marked the first ascent of Everest from its North side. Chinese propaganda claimed that the three members reached the summit – Wang Fuzhou, Qu Yinhua and (the Tibetan) Gonpo – and left a bust, flag and small note there. With no photographic evidence of the ascent, the Chinese announcement was met with scepticism in the West (though it has since been accepted as genuine).

Above: **The Chinese Dream**. A poster from 2013 showing Xi Jinping against a busy background, including doves, a satellite, rockets, a low sun over the Great Wall, military forces, and the Liaoning – China's first aircraft carrier. To the left are the Senkaku Islands, an uninhabited territory long-contested between China and Japan. Xi has occupied the position of General Secretary of the Communist Party since 2012, and President of the People's Republic since 2013. Under Xi, China's foreign policy has grown more assertive, particularly in regards to territorial claims. In late 2012 the Japanese government purchased three of the contested islands from their private owners, prompting widespread protest in China (possibly the catalyst for their inclusion on this poster).

Right: **Uphold science, eradicate superstition**. A poster published in 1999. The poster appeared (alongside others) in a government campaign against the 'cult' of Falun Gong, an anti-communist, ultra-conservative religious movement that rejects the modern scientific principles of evolution and medicine. Founded in the early 1990s by autocratic leader Li Hongzhi, Falun Gong was banned in China in 1999, and many thousands of its adherents were subsequently extrajudicially imprisoned and subjected to various forms of abuse. The movement is currently headquartered in New York and has become notorious for promoting conspiracy theories and far-right politicians.

崇尚科学 破除迷信

Croatian poster from the Second World War (1943) showing a giant deep-sea magnet sucking dozens of spiralling ships down to the bottom of the ocean. No publisher indicated, though possibly issued by Germany to celebrate U-boat successes in the Atlantic and elsewhere. Croatia at the time was Axis-aligned under the Independent State of Croatia (NDH), which was installed in 1941 following the German–Italian invasion.

Cover of *Tricontinental* magazine (see p17), 1969, with intersecting portraits of Ho Chi Minh and Che Guevara, designed by Alfredo Rostgaard. *Tricontinental* was the main publication of the Organization of Solidarity with the People of Asia, Africa and Latin America (or OSPAAAL), which had been founded in 1966 following the Tricontinental Conference. The magazine closely covered anti-colonial movements from around the world, with Vietnam predictably receiving special focus in the late 60s.

Day of the Heroic Guerrilla. A poster published by the Organization of Solidarity with the People of Asia, Africa and Latin America (OSPAAAL). The poster shows multiple images of Che Guevara against a pink background with South America picked out in yellow. The Día del Guerrillero Heroico, celebrated every 8 October since 1968, marks the anniversary of Che's capture by Bolivian forces in 1967 (he was executed the next day).

Liberty or death! The front cover of a children's book published in the early 1960s, not long after the Cuban revolution. The book provides an account of key episodes from the war as well as outlining the main protagonists of the revolution, including Fidel Castro (1926–2016), their leader, who became prime minister from 1959 to 1976, then President from 1976 to 2008. The cover shows a battle scene, with Castro at the top and several other commanders below him. In the middle is Camilo Cienfuegos (1932–1959), a senior guerrilla leader during the revolution and an official hero in Castro's Cuba. To his left is Che Guevara (1928–1967), the globally recognisable guerrilla leader, who was captured and executed by Bolivian Special Forces. On the far left is Faure Chomón (1929–2019), another prominent communist who in 1957, during the dictatorship of Fulgencio Batista, led an assault on the Presidential Palace. Raúl Castro, Fidel's brother, is depicted on the right.

9 May 1945. This postcard (c.1946), illustrated by Czech artist Otto Ušák, was apparently published privately along with several others depicting similar scenes. It celebrates the arrival of the Red Army in Prague on 9 May 1945. A Red Army soldier stands on a torn Nazi flag while offering his hand to a kneeling woman wearing the coat of arms of Bohemia and Moravia, with Prague Castle in the background. The Prague Uprising had taken place four days earlier, allowing the Red Army to subsequently enter the city almost entirely unopposed, suffering very few casualties. The uprising had received unexpected support from the Russian Liberation Army, the previously German-allied, anti-Soviet force led by Andrey Vlasov. During the communist period, Victory Day was celebrated on 9 May every year in Czechoslovakia.

Estonia's answer to Moscow. The Bolsheviks can attack us if they want – we will defend our homeland to the last! This Nazi German propaganda poster urges Estonians to fight against the USSR. Initially neutral in the Second World War, the independent Republic of Estonia was invaded by the Red Army in 1940. After fighting a guerrilla war against the Soviets, the country was subsequently occupied by the Germans between 1941 and 1944, during which time thousands of Estonians were conscripted into the German armed forces.

Danger threatens from the sky! All citizens to defence. A poster published in the 1930s by the Finnish Gas Protection Society (SKJ). In the 1920s, Finland began preparing for the possibility of a future war involving poisonous gases. The SKJ – Suomen Kaasusuojelujärjestö – was founded in 1930 as part of a wider proliferation of civil defence organisations. The SKJ's mission was to educate the population to the dangers of a potential 'gas war', especially with the Soviet Union, and to encourage readiness.

Communism. Socialism. Danger looms! Agrarian League saves. A poster published by the Maalaisliitto (Agrarian League) party showing lightning bolts of communism and socialism threatening a small rural homestead. The threat from the left was a common theme in the party's propaganda material after the Second World War. This image was likely produced for the 1951 election in which Maalaisliitto came second to the Social Democratic Party. They were renamed Suomen Keskusta (Centre Party) in 1965.

le sourire du **COCO**dile.

...est actuellement sa meilleure **arm**

PAIX ET LIBERTÉ

The smile of the COCOdile ... is currently its greatest weapon. This anti-communist poster from around 1950, shows a grinning crocodile with hammer-and-sickle eyes. *Coco* is French slang for 'commie' (communist). It was issued by Paix et Liberté (Peace and Liberty), an organisation established in 1950 to campaign against the French Communist Party (PCF). The majority of its propaganda agitated explicitly against communism, often encouraging voters to avoid the PCF, though a significant amount stressed the importance of European unity, especially as the Marshall Plan (the US economic plan to assist in the rebuilding of Europe after the Second World War, which also secured American political influence across the region) was being rolled out in the late 1940s and early 1950s.

Paix et Liberté was at its most active in the early 1950s when, with US backing, it produced hundreds of thousands of posters, leaflets and films, attacking communism, as well as establishing a radio show hosted by the organisation's founder, Jean-Paul David. At the time the US was supporting similar anti-communist groups across Europe (a notable example being the Volksbund für Frieden und Freiheit in West Germany) to discourage support for communist parties, which were still performing well in European elections. This poster would become one of Paix et Liberté's most enduring designs.

United Europe, guarantee of peace. A poster published in 1951 by the anti-communist Paix et Liberté group, showing a young girl taking cover from the impending Soviet downpour, under a European-flag umbrella. In the decade following the Second World War, Paix et Liberté published huge quantities of anti-communist posters in France, as well as producing a number of propaganda films (with the backing of the US).

NO! France will not be a colonised country! Americans to America! French anti-American poster, 1950, showing the American octopus with dollar-symbol eyes invading France. The poster was issued by the French Communist Party (PCF) and at the bottom reads: 'This poster was paid for by funds collected by Renault factory workers.' The PCF, along with other European communist parties, was at the time publishing a great amount of material denouncing increasing American influence and interference in European affairs.

N'êtes-vous donc pas jolie?

Dévoilez-vous!

Aren't you pretty then? Unveil yourself! A 1957 poster from the Algerian War (1954–1962) urging Muslim women to remove their veils, presumably in part to aid identification. The poster was produced by the Fifth Bureau, the French government's psychological warfare branch, created in the aftermath of the Battle of Algiers. The war began in 1954, when the National Liberation Front (FLN) launched a series of attacks in what was then French Algeria. The conflict gradually grew into a war of independence that would last until 1962, culminating in success for Algeria. The Fifth Bureau was responsible for publishing and disseminating the government's propaganda material between 1957 and 1960, when it was disbanded.

Against the dictatorship in Argentina – no football in the concentration camps. This poster from 1978 calls for an international boycott of the Argentinian World Cup in protest at the country's recently installed military junta. Designed by Jean-François Batellier, it shows the World Cup's logo at the end of barbed-wire fencing and was published by the Committee for the Boycott of the World Cup in Argentina (COBA), which had been founded in Paris a year earlier to agitate against Argentina's hosting of the tournament. The poster was one of many produced by both individuals and organisations worldwide calling for a boycott of the World Cup (in response, the junta and its supporters produced their own propaganda, one example being a booklet from the same year titled 'Argentina and its Human Rights', which defended the junta against accusations of human rights abuses).

A poster from the civil unrest period of 1968, designed anonymously and published by the Atelier Populaire (Popular Workshop), which had been formed by students at the Ecole des Beaux Arts. This one shows a policeman with an 'SS' riot shield – the artist equating the French CRS (Compagnies Républicaines de Securité) to the German Nazi Party's SS (Schutzstaffel). The school was occupied by students and teachers, and was utilised as a studio for the production of protest posters. These were distributed free of charge and pasted up across Paris, acting as a means of conveying both political messages and practical plans of action.

Above: **Sleepless Nights**. First World War postcard (c.1915). A zeppelin airship flies above the head of a gigantic German soldier as he peers through a window into the bedroom of Marianne (the embodiment of the French Republic, representing the values of 'Liberty, Equality and Fraternity').

Right: Berlin's 'Iron Hindenburg', a wooden sculpture of Paul von Hindenburg, who had become a national hero after winning the 1914 Battle of Tannenberg against the Russians, followed by a string of subsequent victories on the Eastern Front. One of the so-called *Nagelmänner* ('Nail Men') erected in Germany and Austria during the First World War for both propaganda and fundraising purposes. The practice originated in Vienna, where the first

Nail Man was built in March 1915 in the form of a wooden knight, into which the public was invited to hammer nails in return for a donation. Known as the *Wehrmann im Eisen* (Soldier in Iron), the figure still stands outside the Vienna *Rathaus* (City Hall) today.

'Iron Hindenburg', the largest and most famous of the Nail Men, was unveiled in September 1915. The ceremony was attended by prominent figures such as Princess Alexandra Victoria and Chancellor Theobald von Bethmann Hollweg, who delivered a speech, and along with the princess, hammered the first nails into the sculpture. Within hours, the number of nails had reached tens of thousands (and by August 1918 it was almost a million). The sculpture drew the attention of the international press and spawned mocking imitations in Allied countries, most notably in Britain.

ZEICHNET
KRIEGS-ANLEIHE
FÜR U-BOOTE GEGEN
ENGLAND

Purchase war loans for U-boats against England. This postcard from the
First World War (1914) shows Britain surrounded by submarines. It was
published at the start of Germany's U-boat campaign, which was launched
in August 1914, principally against the British Grand Fleet. By the beginning
of 1915, Germany had adopted the tactic of targeting merchant ships in an
effort to strangle Britain's economy.

KAMPF um NORWEGEN

Ein Erinnerungsblatt an den Feldzug 1940

This poster from the Second World War shows a colossal German soldier standing guard over a serene Norwegian landscape. It was published to promote the 1940 propaganda documentary *Kampf um Norwegen – Feldzug 1940* (*Battle for Norway – 1940 Campaign*), which details events leading up to the invasion of Norway, arguing that the Germans were forced to invade because of increasing British aggression. The film was never shown in Germany and was considered lost until 2005, when Jostein Saakvitne, a Norwegian professor, discovered a copy listed on an internet auction site.

A brochure protesting Germany's hosting of the 1936 Summer Olympics. Produced by German exiles and published in Paris, the cover shows an athlete throwing a javelin while his shadow is in the form of a gas-masked soldier throwing a *Stielhandgranate* (stick hand grenade). Nazi militarism, race policies and political persecution often featured as themes in propaganda calling for an international boycott of the Berlin Olympics.

The enemy sees your light! Blackout! A poster from the Second World War (c.1942) showing a skeleton riding a British plane at night, preparing to throw a bomb down on a brightly lit house below. Designed by Otto Sander-Herweg and published in Dresden by the Deutsche Propaganda Atelier, it was one of many similar posters issued by both sides during the war, urging citizens to use blackouts as a means of combatting air raids.

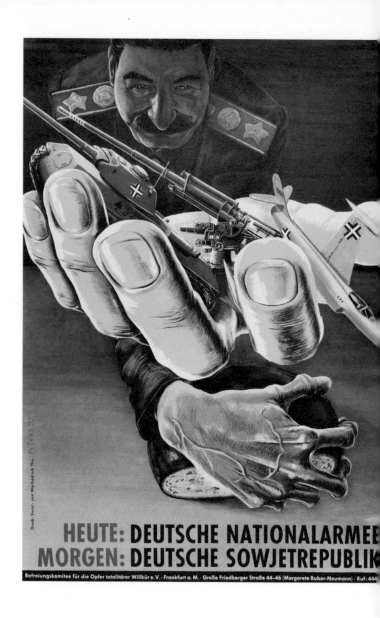

HEUTE: DEUTSCHE NATIONALARMEE
MORGEN: DEUTSCHE SOWJETREPUBLIK

Befreiungskomitee für die Opfer totalitärer Willkür e. V. · Frankfurt a. M. · Große Friedberger Straße 44-46 (Margarete Buber-Neumann) · Ruf: 444

Today: German National Army, Tomorrow: German Soviet Republic (1952).
A ghoulish Stalin offers military equipment with one hand, while stealing
bread with the other. This West German poster published by the 'Liberation
Committee for the Victims of Totalitarian Tyranny' was produced in response
to Stalin's 1952 proposal for German unification, which many in West Germany
interpreted as a ploy to increase Soviet influence over the country.

INTERNATIONALER
FRAUENTAG
8. MÄRZ 1955

International Women's Day. An East German poster published in 1955 showing a woman wearing a headscarf decorated with the countries of the world (though predominantly European). Women's Day began in Europe in 1911 after Clara Zetkin and Käte Duncker (both German communists and women's rights activists) proposed the idea at the 1910 International Socialist Women's Conference in Copenhagen. The day was supported by various socialist and communist parties, who often published posters announcing speeches, protests and other events. Over time, it became closely associated with communist groups, causing it to be banned in Germany from 1933 until the end of the Second World War. In 1947 it was officially reinstated in the East, developing into one of the most prominent occasions of the year in the German Democratic Republic.

Above: **Under the banner of Karl Marx, for peace and social progress!** Poster, East Berlin, 1983.

Right: **STOP Yankee beetles**. An East German pamphlet published in 1950 showing beetles, branded with the American Stars and Stripes, charging along a racetrack. The text on the left reads **Documents on the Colorado beetle drop** – a reference to the accusation from the DDR that the US had airdropped the potato pest over East German fields, in an attempt to sabotage the East German economy. The beetle had been present in Europe since the late nineteenth century after being introduced through imported crops. In June 1950, less than a year after the DDR's official establishment, an East German farmer reported that his crops had been infested by the potato beetle after two American planes had flown over his fields. The authorities were

quick to blame the infestations on a US conspiracy, with propaganda referring to the beetles as *Amikäfer* (Yankee beetles). Posters and pamphlets like this one depicted the Amikäfer as colossal, American-branded beetles, waging war against the crops, while children's schoolbooks showed citizens combing through the fields collecting as many of the pests as they could to be destroyed. In neighbouring Poland, the authorities also began to denounce 'the crimes of the American pilots, who dropped tremendous amounts of the potato beetle on the fields of the German Democratic Republic.' The idea of a weaponised potato beetle wasn't entirely new or implausible: during the First World War both the British and French had considered dropping them over Germany.

Vote down EDA. An anti-communist poster from the 1958 election, showing the Soviet octopus stretching its tentacles across Greece. Its eyes are labelled 'KKE' (Communist Party of Greece) and 'EDA' (United Democratic Left), and its cap 'USSR'. It is likely the poster was produced by the anti-communist journal *Sovietology*, run by George Georgalas, a former communist who later worked for the Ministry of Public Relations and Propaganda under the military junta that seized power in 1967. Despite abundant anti-communist propaganda the EDA performed well in elections: by 1958 they were the second largest party in the Greek parliament behind the right-wing National Radical Union. However, following the 1967 coup, the EDA was outlawed.

Hail victory. A poster from the Metaxas period of 1936–1941, when Greece was governed by the dictator General Ioannis Metaxas, under his 4th of August Regime. This poster was produced to promote the National Youth Organisation (EON) whose logo appears bottom right. The top left reads '4th of August', the date that Metaxas suspended the Greek parliament and took power. Elements of the regime were modelled on fascist Italy, but Metaxas cited Portugal's *Estado Novo* (New State) as his main influence. The regime had its own uniforms, culture and rituals, including the Roman (fascist) salute (shown here) which Metaxas believed to be Greek in origin.

PROTECT YOURSELF. A poster from c.1970 designed by György Pál. Initially he was employed to produce commercial posters for products such as soap, light bulbs, etc. During the Second World War, Hungary was occupied by the Soviet Red Army. With the advent of the communist regime in 1948, Pál was regularly commissioned to design socialist posters on topics ranging from livestock to civil defence (as with this example). The text below reads: 'It's our shared cause – our shared interest. The most important task of the Civil Defence is to save human lives.'

How to return our disabled to life. Published during the First World War (1915), this poster shows a soldier with a prosthetic arm working with a scythe. Designed by Lajos Csabai Ékes and Árpád Ékes (who collaborated on a number of posters during the war) it advertises a documentary by Hungarian cinematographer Jenő Illés concerning advances in medical treatment, particularly prosthetics, for soldiers injured in combat. Largely recorded in hospitals around Budapest, the film premiered in that city in January 1916.

Let's march to Delhi! A Second World War poster (c.1943) promoting the Indian National Army (INA). Their leader, Subhas Chandra Bose, stands over India; behind him INA troops march in formation carrying the 'springing tiger' flag of the Azad Hind, or Provisional Government of Free India. Formed in occupied Singapore in 1943 the Azad Hind received considerable support from Japan. The figures top left are Mahatma Gandhi (anti-colonial nationalist campaigner) and Jawaharlal Nehru (anti-colonial nationalist and statesman). The text at the bottom is a quote from Subhas Chandra Bose (a nationalist allied with Axis forces): 'Give me your blood, I will give you freedom.' Under the marching column (top right) are the Andaman and Nicobar Islands, which Bose renamed the Martyr and Self-rule Islands.

सुभाष बलिदान

Subhas's sacrifice. A print from 1948 showing nationalist leader Subhas Chandra Bose offering his head to Mother India (Bharat Mata) as she subdues the raging British dragon. The severed heads of other nationalist and independence leaders are scattered below. At the top, Bose is depicted next to Delhi's Red Fort, which flies the Indian flag. During the war Bose led the Azad Hind (Provisional Government of Free India) against the British. Aligning with Axis forces, he led the Indian National Army against the Allies in Burma and elsewhere, before retreating East in 1945. He died on 18 August 1945 when the Japanese plane in which he was travelling crashed in Taiwan. Various rumours and conspiracy theories circulated immediately after his death, which was regarded as suspicious by his followers.

The powerful army is the protector of independence and pride of each Iranian. This army poster, c.1950s, was published during the reign of Shah Mohammed Reza Pahlavi. It depicts a soldier set against the outline of Iran and the former Iranian flag (the 'Lion and Sun' symbol was abandoned in 1980 and replaced by the National Emblem of Iran). The design appears to have been influenced by posters produced during the Spanish Civil War.

The Shah's exile and Khomeini's return. A 1979 poster depicting events of the Iranian Revolution in which the Shah (the last monarch) was overthrown. Ayatollah Khomeini holds the Quran aloft, while a crowd marches below him. In the background, Iraq's Najaf Shrine and the Eiffel Tower allude to Khomeini's period of exile. The Devil watches as the Shah flees the country with his black dog companion. Carrying briefcases overflowing with American and British money, he crosses the Persian Gulf, evading a noose. Iran itself is in turmoil: protestors tear down a statue of the Shah, soldiers shoot at a crowd, tanks demolish buildings and revolutionaries execute prisoners.

Disastrous U.S. missile attack against Iranian airliner. A stamp, issued in August 1988, depicting the downing of Iran Air Flight 655. The passenger plane had been shot down on 3 July by surface-to-air missiles fired from the American warship USS *Vincennes*. All 290 passengers and crew were killed, prompting international outcry and making the attack the subject of much Iranian propaganda. The incident took place during the Iran–Iraq War (1980–1988) in which international merchant shipping had come under fire. After stating that the airliner had been mistaken for an Iranian jet fighter, the US government paid nearly 62 million dollars in compensation.

Our revolutionary guard does not belong only to our brothers in the armed forces. Men and women, young and old in our country are the members of the Islamic Army, and are the guardians of Islam. A poster from 1979 showing a young girl holding a Kalashnikov with a flower in the barrel. The quote is from Mahmoud Taleghani, a prominent leader during the revolution of 1979 against the Shah (see p77).

This painting from 1999 shows Saddam Hussein as an ancient Mesopotamian king on a lion hunt. Murals and posters were a common sight throughout Saddam's Iraq, but pieces like this were often especially commissioned for rallies, parades and other state occasions, as well as for use in palaces. This painting was made for Maqar-el-Tharthar, Saddam's newly built resort on Tharthar Lake. The largest and most elaborate of his palaces, it was constructed for his 62nd birthday. Saddam was often depicted in Iraqi propaganda as an ancient Mesopotamian king, stressing continuity between antiquity and modernity.

A mural (c.1987) showing Saddam Hussein marching into combat with faded, dreamlike images of children and national landmarks (such as the Ishtar Gate) behind him and the Iraqi army at his flank – as if he were the only truly solid reality in the whole country. One of the more famous Saddam-era murals, it was apparently painted and displayed at Al-Mustansiriyah University's College of Arts in Baghdad. Images of Saddam personally leading his army into battle became more common in Iraqi propaganda throughout the 1990s, one especially common theme being that of Saddam leading his forces in a march on Jerusalem.

WANTED

THE MOTHER

الوَجْهُ البَارِدُ للمَوْتِ وَالحَرْبِ

OF ALL EVIL

The cold face of death and war. A British psychological operations (PSYOP) leaflet from 1990. During the Gulf War (1990–1991) anti-Saddam Hussein leaflets such as this one were dropped over Iraqi troop positions. In 1991, 87,000 Iraqi troops surrendered, thanks in part to such propaganda. Saddam's Ba'athist government were overthown in 2003 during the Iraq War (2003–2011) and he was executed in 2006 for crimes against humanity. The leaflet is held in the collection of the Imperial War Museum in London.

Baghdad, 2004. A portrait of Saddam Hussein, riddled with bullet holes, being painted over at a former training camp for the Fedayeen – a paramilitary group operating outside the law, loyal to (and willing to sacrifice themselves for) Saddam's government. They reported directly to the Presidential Palace, rather than the military, and were responsible for some of the most brutal acts of the regime.

Growth versus siege! This poster published c.1950 shows an Arab soldier looming over Israel, while thousands of immigrants arrive by boat. It was published by the Mapai Party, winners of the country's first election in 1949, with its leader, David Ben-Gurion, becoming the first Prime Minister. Mapai would dominate Israeli politics for the next two decades and, as suggested in this poster, national defence was its foremost preoccupation, along with economic and population growth. After the Arab-Israeli War of 1948, hundreds of thousands of Palestinians were expelled from their homes, with no right of return. Meanwhile, hundreds of thousands of Jews emigrated to Israel in the early years of its existence, including 260,000 expelled from the surrounding Arab territories. Tensions remained high with neighbouring countries, particularly Egypt, and the prospect of war remained.

זרקים

התנדב לצנחנים!

Volunteer for the paratroopers! A recruitment poster from the 1950s showing Israeli paratroopers descending toward the ground, the nearest under a parachute in the form of a military beret. The maroon beret was a distinctive part of the uniform of the newly founded Paratroopers Brigade (officially the 35th Brigade), which had been established in 1955 as an elite assault force. Its first commander was Ariel Sharon (1928–2014), who later became Prime Minister of Israel (2001–2006). In its first year the brigade mostly carried out raids behind enemy lines in neighbouring territory, in particular Gaza, Sinai and Syria. Paratroopers played an important role during the Suez conflict of 1956 and the Six-Day War of 1967. During the latter they fought on several fronts in Egypt, Syria, the West Bank and Jerusalem.

ירושלים
על הכוונת!

Jerusalem, I have you in my sights! This poster from 1994 shows Yasser Arafat, the then leader of the Palestine Liberation Organization (PLO), aiming a gun directly out at us. It was published alongside several other designs as part of an anti-PLO campaign that ran during the negotiations between the PLO and the Israeli government of Yitzhak Rabin (1922–1995). The negotiations included breakthroughs such as the Madrid Conference of 1991, and later the Oslo Accords of 1993. Rabin was assassinated in 1995 by Yigal Amir, a right-wing extremist who opposed the Oslo Accords.

Vote vav [the Hebrew letter 'vav'. Each politial party has a designated letter].
The Black Panthers, Hadash. The Israeli Black Panthers protest movement
was founded in 1971 with the aim of working in the interests of Sephardi
and Mizrahi Jews. This poster from 1977 urges voters to support the newly
formed Hadash party, Israel's leftist coalition, in that year's elections.

Enough! A cartoon from 1924, showing the word *BASTA* breaking a fascist in half, a commentary on the murder of Giacomo Matteotti, who was kidnapped and killed by fascists after he alleged they had committed fraud in the general election of that year. It was published in *L'Asino* (The Donkey) magazine, a satirical, left-wing weekly publication that ran from 1892 to 1925. *L'Asino* was forced to close because of increasing restrictions and harassment by the dictatorship of fascist Prime Minister, Benito Mussolini. The cartoon was drawn by Gabriele Galantara, journalist, illustrator and co-founder of *L'Asino*. After the closure of the magazine he continued to make cartoons for other publications until his imprisonment by the regime in 1926.

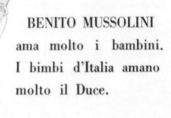

BENITO MUSSOLINI
ama molto i bambini.
I bimbi d'Italia amano
molto il Duce.

VIVA IL DUCE!

Un saluto al Duce.

54

Benito Mussilini loves children very much. The children of Italy are very fond of Il Duce. Long live Il Duce! Greetings to Il Duce. Portrait of Mussolini from an Italian children's book of the 1930s.

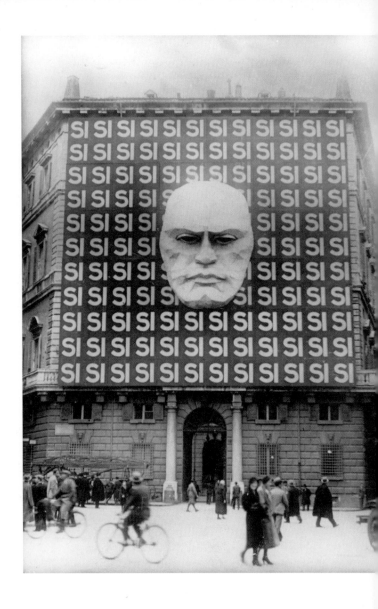

A huge likeness of Benito Mussolini stares down on the citizens of Rome from the facade of the Palazzo Braschi (1934). Behind his image the word **SI** (YES) is repeated, a reminder that people should vote for him in the upcoming election.

YES. Published during the 1934 general election, in the *Rivista illustrata del popolo d'Italia* (*The Illustrated Magazine of the Italian People*, founded by Benito Mussolini in 1914). This collage, designed by the Swiss painter and designer Xanti Schawinsky, shows Mussolini's body formed from a crowd, while the 'SI' letters contain electoral scenes and statistics.

Mussolini's National Fascist Party (PNF) was the sole political party at the time of the election, essentially a referendum on the PNF's legitimacy. Voters were asked: 'Do you approve the list of members appointed by the Grand National Council of Fascism?' Some 99.85 per cent voted 'yes', leading Mussolini to dub the election the 'second referendum of Fascism' (the first having been held in 1929 returning 98.43 per cent in favour).

...e la morte a paro a paro

A postcard from the Second World War (1941) showing Death guiding a naked, dagger-wielding aviator descending through the sky along with aeroplanes and parachutists, with the line at the bottom quoting from Gabriele D'Annunzio's poem 'La canzone del Quarnaro' ('...and death at my side'). It celebrates the 185th Paratroopers Division *Folgore* ('Thunderbolt'), which was founded in September 1941 and deployed to North Africa, to fight in the Western Desert campaign in Libya and Egypt. The division was largely wiped out the following year during the Second Battle of El Alamein. The signature top right reads 'Berthelet', an artist who designed a series of postcards for the Italian military at the start of the war.

MADONNINA DEL DUOMO · DI MILANO GLORIA ·
L'ITALIA IN ARMI CONDUCI ALLA VITTORIA!

Madonnina del Duomo, glory of Milan, lead Italy to victory! A postcard from the Second World War (1941) showing the Madonnina of Milan leading ships and planes across the sea. (The real sculpture of the Madonnina – a symbol of the city – sits atop the tallest spire of the Milan cathedral.)

Above: Sputnik-themed car used by the Italian Communist Party (PCI) during the 1958 general election. In the previous year, the Soviet Union had launched the first artificial Earth satellite, Sputnik 1. Much of the PCI election material promoted this achievement as a great feat of communism.

Right: **No! Neither fascism nor communism, vote Christian–Democracy**. A poster from the 1948 general election published by the Christian Democracy party. It shows a communist arm (with the hammer and sickle symbol) giving the raised fist salute and a fascist arm (with the fasces symbol) giving the raised arm salute. Christian Democracy were a centrist party that won the election decisively, thanks in part to a massive propaganda campaign backed by the US and Great Britain (as well as the Catholic Church), who were fearful of a gradual communist takeover of Italy. The party's shield emblem (at the bottom right of the design) often appeared on their published material. The many hundreds of posters produced in the run up to the election, both by Christian Democracy and its rivals, are among the most memorable of the immediate postwar era.

Russian Bears versus Rising Sun. This postcard from 1905 celebrates Japanese victory in the Russo-Japanese War, the design showing Russian bears (carrying the flag of the Imperial Navy) put into disarray by powerful beams emitted from the eyes of the rising sun. War had broken out in February 1904 following territorial disputes in Manchuria and Korea. Japan quickly gained the upper hand with a series of victories, although the conflict dragged on until September 1905, when it was finally brought to an end with the Treaty of Portsmouth, an agreement brokered by US President Theodore Roosevelt. The postcard was one of a set celebrating the Japanese victory.

A Second World War leaflet from 1942, showing a Japanese soldier using the heads of American and British soldiers as stepping stones, with a Dutch soldier in the background. The text commemorates the first anniversary of the 'Greater East Asian War' (the Japanese name for both the war with the Allies and the ongoing war in China) and the people of Asia 'cutting off their chains'. The Japanese entered the Second World War on 7 December 1941, with simutaneous attacks on several American bases (including Pearl Harbor) alongside the invasion of Thailand, Malaya, Singapore and Hong Kong.

A postcard from the Second World War (c.1941) showing a pilot tying a rising sun *hachimaki* (headband) around his head. Worn as a symbol of courage, *hachimaki* are often associated with *kamikaze* ('divine wind') pilots, who were trained to undertake suicide missions, deliberately flying their planes into Allied warships in order to destroy them. The first units were formed in 1944, and by the end of the Pacific campaign in 1945, around 3,800 *kamikaze* pilots had died, killing over 7,000 naval personnel, sinking 34 ships and damaging 368 others. The subject of this illustration, however, is apparently not a *kamikaze*. It is based on a famous photograph taken in 1940 of navy pilot Hideo Oishi, flying with the 12th Kokutai (air group) in China.

The cover of *The Third World War*, a Japanese video game released in 1993, showing Saddam Hussein and Bill Clinton shaking hands while an apocalyptic war unfolds around them. In this turn-based strategy game, each player chooses to act as a particular nation, attempting to prevent total global war, while simultaneously working towards either military or economic victories. (The nations included in the game are: America, United Kingdom, Russia, Japan, Germany, China, France, India, Brazil, Canada, Australia, Iraq, Israel, Saudi Arabia, South Africa and Libya.)

المقاومة الوطنية اللبنانية
(وزارة الجنوب)

We will resist. A poster published by the Lebanese National Resistance Front (LRNF) at the start of the Lebanon War (1982–1985). The poster shows a man defiant in front of several Star of David-branded gun barrels. It is one of the most well-known propaganda pieces from the period. The Israel–Lebanon border had witnessed years of back-and-forth violence between the Palestine Liberation Organization (PLO) operating in southern Lebanon and the Israeli military. The attempted assassination of the Israeli ambassador to the United Kingdom by a splinter group of the PLO was used as the catalyst for the invasion. Ultimately the PLO were forced to withdraw to Tripoli and then Tunisia.

A Cuban poster published in 1983 by the Organization of Solidarity with the People of Asia, Africa and Latin America (OSPAAAL). This was one of many produced by OSPAAAL during the Cold War, expressing solidarity with revolutionary countries, movements and leaders around the world. Designed by Alberto Blanco.

This 1988 postcard shows the Libyan ruler Muammar Gaddafi (1942–2011) trying to protect children from US airstrikes. It is part of a set issued with a series of stamps, to mark the 'Second Anniversary of American Aggression'. This refers to the US bombing raids of 15 April 1986, carried out in retaliation for the bombing of a West Berlin nightclub frequented by American soldiers ten days earlier, which Ronald Reagan blamed on Gaddafi. Gaddafi claimed that his adopted daughter, Hana, was killed during the strikes.

Africa belongs to Africans. A poster featuring Muammar Gaddafi outside the Bab al-Bahr ('Sea Gate') Hotel in Tripoli, 2000. Gaddafi's attempts to establish a United Arab Republic (between Libya, Egypt and Syria) had been frustrated. Instead, he turned to pan-Africanism, calling for an economic and political union of African countries named the United States of Africa. In 2009 he was crowned 'King of Kings' by a group of traditional African leaders, and subsequently elected as chair of the African Union.

A portrait of Muammar Gaddafi on the side of a large balloon. The photograph was taken in Tripoli, Libya, in 1991 during celebrations for the 22nd anniversary of Gaddafi's rule. A poster with his portrait is also visible on the building behind. Gaddafi seized power in a 1969 coup, retaining that power for the next four decades, until his overthrow in 2011.

A postcard (c.1970s) showing a photo-montage of Muammar Gaddafi, commander-in-chief of the Libyan armed forces, visiting Mecca. He wears the uniform of a colonel and a Rolex Datejust watch.

$ 1,000/=

凡任何一位馬共人員能
够脫離森林把一挺布連鎗帶
出來,或是帶領保安隊伍去將
他所知道收藏的布連鎗發掘
出來,都可獲得一千元的賞金.

獲得一千元賞金
開始新的生活!

No.1828

Receive a $1,000 reward to start a new life! This leaflet was dropped over communist guerrillas during the Malayan Emergency of 1948–1960, when the Malayan Communist Party fought a guerrilla war against Commonwealth forces. The full text reads: 'If any member of the Malayan Communist Party is able to leave the jungle and bring out a Bren gun, or is able to lead the Peace Keeping Forces to unearth a hidden Bren gun that he or she knows about, he will be eligible for a $1,000 reward.'

'Mexico for Freedom'. A poster published in 1942, the year Mexico joined the Second World War, after two of its merchant ships were torpedoed, sparking public outrage. The image shows an eagle tearing apart a Nazi flag, set against a low sun, with the colours of the Mexican flag in the sky. It was painted by the artist José Bribiesca Ruvalcaba (1915–1959) who produced a broad range of work, from pin-up girls to still lifes.

We are not alone! A poster from the Second World War (c.1943) showing the Mexican flag flying against a background made up of the flags of the Allies. Designed by Julio Prieto for Mexico's Department of Public Education (Secretaría de Educación Pública). Throughout the war Mexico provided support to the Allied war effort, supplying raw materials and labour (hundreds of thousands of temporary farmworkers) as well as the so-called Aztec Eagles air squadron, or Escuadrón 201, that fought alongside the US Air Force in the Philippines.

Study, produce, fight. A Mozambique Liberation Front (FRELIMO) poster from 1973, showing two fighters against a lush, semi-abstract forest background. It was published to mark Revolution Day, celebrating FRELIMO's first military offensive against their colonial rulers, Portugal. FRELIMO was fighting for independence, which it eventually won in 1975. It was then renamed the Frelimo Party and officially declared itself Marxist–Leninist. For the first decade and a half of independence the government fought a civil war against anti-communist insurgents, the Mozambican National Resistance. In 1992, the war ended and the Frelimo Party has ruled the country ever since.

A poster by Reyn Dirksen, c.1950, showing the many-flagged ship of Europe sailing through stormy waters. It was produced for a Marshall Plan poster competition where artists from participating countries were asked to submit designs on the theme of 'Intra-European Cooperation for a Better Standard of Living', promoting European unity and the benefits of American aid. Over 10,000 entries were received, with this one taking first place. The Marshall Plan, officially the European Recovery Programme (ERP), was an American initiative to provide aid to European countries in the wake of the Second World War. The ERP's objective was to rebuild Europe's devastated economies and in doing so guard against growing communist influence.

Poster published by the Communist Party of New Zealand (CPNZ), c.1943, promising community centres, gas, transit housing, parking facilities, playing fields and transport facilities. The CPNZ was founded in 1921 but remained a small party for the entirety of its existence, with its membership peaking at 2,000 in 1945. Never achieving real power or influence, in 1994 it merged with the International Socialist Organisation to form the Socialist Workers Organisation, which itself quickly split into numerous sub-parties.

Death to imperialism. Published by the Sandinista National Liberation Front (FSLN), c.1982, this poster shows Nicaraguan revolutionary Augusto César Sandino (after whom the FSLN is named). Sandino led an uprising against US occupation between 1927 and 1933, subsequently becoming a national symbol of anti-imperial struggle, particularly against the US. The text at the top reads: 'Come, scum of morphine addicts ... I'll make you bite the dust of my wild mountains.'

WANTED
for murder

and torture of
Irish prisoners

This British anti-Thatcher poster (1981) was published during the hunger
strikes in Northern Ireland. The strikes were undertaken by Irish Republican
prisoners between 1980 and 1981 in protest at the government's withdrawal
of their status as political prisoners. Ultimately, ten prisoners died, prompting
international protest and outrage, particularly at the British Prime Minister
Margaret Thatcher, who was condemned by many as being directly responsible
for their deaths. The stike was eventually called off after James Prior, the
new Northern Ireland Secretary, sanctioned limited concessions. The
publisher of the poster is anonymous, but it was reproduced in several
variants around the world, often advertising anti-government protests.

Above: Boy in Belfast, 1970, posing with Sinn Féin's 'Don't Fraternise!' poster. The image of two soliders or policemen standing over an injured civilian has been directly copied from a Mexican poster published during the student protests of 1968.

Right: A Republican poster produced in Northern Ireland during the Troubles (c.1974), alerting locals to the presence of British intelligence officers. The illustration shows a man divided in two, one half dressed as a British soldier on patrol, the other as a civilian down the pub, with the text at the bottom reading: 'Watch what you say.' 'The Troubles' was the collective name for the long conflict over the status of Northern Ireland, lasting from the late 1960s to 1998. Unionists and loyalists (mostly Ulster Protestants) wanted the territory to remain in the United Kingdom and Irish nationalists and republicans (mostly Irish Catholics) wanted to leave to join a united Ireland. The poster publisher is simply named as 'Republican Movement'.

THIS
GUNMAN - -

A double-sided leaflet (see opposite for reverse) issued in Northern Ireland in 1974, during the Troubles (lasting from the late 1960s to 1998) warning parents of the dangers of allowing their children to play with toy guns. In August 1969 troops had been deployed to Northern Ireland by the British

—IS PLAYING - WITH DEATH

TOY GUNS CAN EASILY BE MISTAKEN FOR REAL GUNS.
DON'T RISK YOUR CHILD'S LIFE.
STOP HIM PLAYING WITH TOY GUNS IN THE STREET

Issued by the Security Forces.

government as a peacekeeping force. However, the situation quickly deteriorated and the army became involved in a prolonged engagement, only being completely withdrawn in 2007. Between 1969 and 1998 3,489 people were killed as a result of the conflict, of which 274 were under 18.

A Republican mural on Ballymurphy Road, Belfast, Northern Ireland, 1992. The painting depicts (left to right): a soldier of the Irish Republican Army, Irish revolutionary James Connolly, Mexican revolutionary Emiliano Zapata, and a Black Panther member. The Irish flag backdrop is painted with a banner at the top showing the phoenix (adopted as a symbol of the Provisional IRA's 'rebirth' in 1969); underneath is the Aztec eagle emblem of the United Farm Workers union in America. The text reads: 'You can kill the revolutionary but not the revolution.'

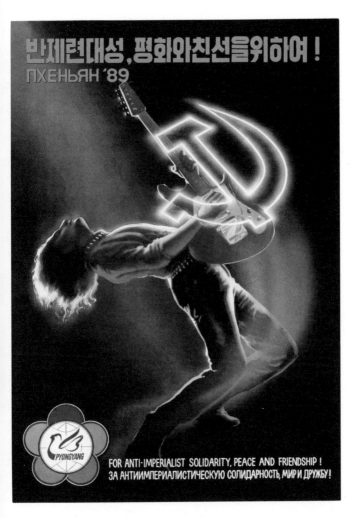

반제련대성, 평화와친선을위하여 !
ПХЕНЬЯН '89

PYONGYANG

FOR ANTI-IMPERIALIST SOLIDARITY, PEACE AND FRIENDSHIP !
ЗА АНТИИМПЕРИАЛИСТИЧЕСКУЮ СОЛИДАРНОСТЬ, МИР И ДРУЖБУ !

For anti-imperialist solidarity, peace and friendship! A promotional poster for the 13th World Festival of Youth and Students, taking place in Pyongyang, in 1989. Organised by the World Federation of Democratic Youth, the festival brought together 22,000 people from around the world to participate in discussions relating to 'Independence and national liberation struggles', 'Peace', and 'Environmental crisis' (among other subjects). Alongside this, the festival also included rock and disco events. It was held bi-annually during the Cold War, almost exclusively in communist countries. The Pyongyang World Festival was the last before the collapse of the Soviet Union and the Eastern Bloc – it was not until 1997 that the next would take place, in Cuba. Since then, the festival has only been held sporadically.

A painting (undated) showing Kim Jong-il overseeing the production of *Sea of Blood* (1969). The black and white film, lasting four hours and twenty minutes, uses graphic violence to tell the story of heroine Sun-Nyo and her family, as she joins the communist revolution to fight against Japan's brutal occupation of Korea in the 1930s. Espousing the national principal of 'Juche'

(the official state ideology of North Korea), it has also been adapted into an opera (1971) and a novel (1973). Kim documented his opinion of what made a compelling film in his book *On the Art of Cinema* (1973), where he outlined his ideas on the most effective (hence permitted) methods of filmmaking. The painting is displayed in Pyongyang Film Studio.

Two stills taken from a video aired on Korean Central Television on 25 March 2022, showing Kim Jong-un overseeing the launch of the Hwasong-17 intercontinental ballistic missile (ICBM). The largest ICBM in the world, with the potential to deliver a nuclear warhead to any US target, it was first revealed in Pyongyang in October 2020 during a ceremony held for the 75th anniversary of the Workers' Party of Korea. Kim hailed the successful test of the so-called 'monster missile' as 'miraculous', remarking that it was a 'priceless' victory for the Korean people.

The Liberator of Korea painted by Vladivostok-based artist Vasily Galaktionov.
Kim Jong-un is shown on horseback trampling the American and South
Korean flags. The Arch of Reunification, built in 2001 to celebrate Korean
unification proposals, is visible in the background. The painting was presented
to Kim by Anatoly Dolgachev in 2013, on the occasion of his birthday.
Dolgachev, a communist legislator in Russia's Primorsky territory, is also
chairman of the 'Far Eastern Association for the Study of the Juche Idea'
(Juche being the official state ideology of North Korea). Reportedly, the
South Korean Consulate in Vladivostok condemned Dolgachev for the gift.

Top: **Let us carry out the first year's tasks under the five-year plan advanced at the Eighth Congress of the Workers' Party of Korea!** Bottom: **All out for the implementation of the decisions made at the Second General Meeting of the Eighth Central Committee of the Workers' Party of Korea!** North Korean posters published in 2021 following a general meeting of the ruling Workers' Party of Korea. They are the result of a collaboration between the Mansudae Art Studio (the biggest producer of North Korean public art with over 4,000 employees), the Korean Federation of Literature and Arts, and the Pyongyang University of Fine Arts, which is the foremost institute for teaching 'Juche-art' (Juche being the official state ideology of North Korea).

Follow us up north! A propaganda poster from the Second World War (1942) by Harald Damsleth (1906–1971) for the Norwegian Ski Ranger Battalion, a unit within the Waffen-SS. Damsleth was a cartoonist and illustrator who also worked in advertising. An early member of the Norwegian Fascist Party, he was once described as a 'specialist on Aryan facial traits'. After producing a vast amount of propaganda (see also p63), he was tried for treason at the end of the war and served two years hard labour.

Above and right: two advertisements placed in the *Pakistani Dawn* newspaper in 1971 during the Indo-Pakistani War. The newspaper, which was founded in 1941 as a mouthpiece for the Muslim League, was the country's largest English language publication and ran dozens of similar print ads calling for total commitment to the war effort. The one above calls on readers to be committed to 'Jehad' (*jihad*: a holy war to defend Islam) and to help fund the war by donating to the National Defence Fund. The advert on the right implores readers to contribute like a *mujahid* (a Muslim engaged in a *jihad*). Both advertisements were sponsored by agricultural companies.

Conflict broke out between the two countries on 3 December 1971 during Bangladesh's War of Independence in what was then East Pakistan. India intervened on the Bangladeshi side in December after Pakistan had launched preemptive strikes on Indian positions. The war lasted just under two weeks, ending with Pakistan's surrender on 16 December 1971.

EXTERMINATE
THE ENEMY
ONCE AND FOR ALL
CONTRIBUTE
LIKE A MUJAHID
TO THE
NATIONAL DEFENCE
FUND

PAKTRACK
KARACHI
LAHORE
DACCA

VICTORY BELONGS TO THOSE WHO FIGHT
FOR A RIGHT CAUSE.
OUR VALIANT ARMED FORCES ARE
DEFENDING THE SACRED SOIL OF
PAKISTAN IN TRUE TRADITION OF THE
WARRIORS OF ISLAM.

INSHA-ALLAH VICTORY IS OURS.

RIZVI BROTHERS LTD.
Rizvi Chambers, Abbar Road, Sader Karachi
Lahore-Dacca-Chittagong.

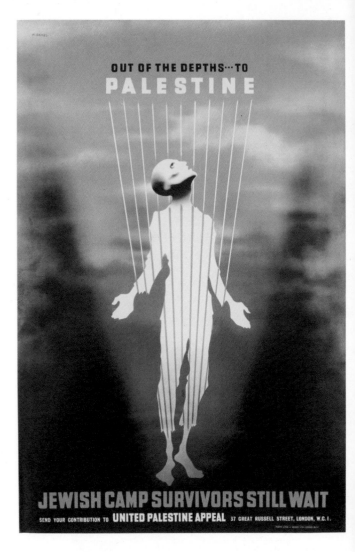

A poster published by the United Palestine Appeal (UPA) in 1945 showing a man wearing a concentration camp uniform, its blue stripes extending as white lines of hope towards the word 'Palestine'. The UPA was founded in 1939 as an umbrella organisation consolidating several other bodies, including the Jewish National Fund, to campaign and fundraise for a Jewish homeland in Palestine. The British were governing what was then known as Mandatory Palestine and attempting to stem the flow of immigrants, largely from post-war refugee camps in Europe. The poster was created by famed graphic designer Abram Games, who felt compelled to produce the work after seeing the first film footage of the Bergen-Belsen concentration camp.

National unity in the face of the enemy. This poster, c.1968, was published by the Vanguard of the Popular Liberation War (Al Sa'iqa) on the day of the Nakba (15 May) when Palestinians remember the displacement of 1948. The rest of the text reads: 'May 15th is the anniversary of a crime that must come to an end. Encourage full Arab support and participation in the struggle. Join with the anti-colonial, anti-Zionist forces. Continuous struggle and total popular revolution.' Al Sa'iqa was founded in 1966 as a Ba'athist group, controlled by Syria as the Palestinian branch of the Syrian Ba'athist Party. In the late 1960s, it joined the Palestine Liberation Organization, struggling alongside Fatah and Yasser Arafat for primacy in the conflict against Israel. Its senior members were purged when Hafez al-Assad became President of Syria in 1970.

The Generation of the Palestinian Revolution. Palestinian poster published by Fatah (Palestinian National Liberation Movement) in c.1985 showing a man and woman, both armed, running gleefully through a field.

Top: **Confessions of a Senderista**. Bottom: **Popular Judgement** – a comic book issued and distributed by the Peruvian government during their decade-long conflict against the communist party of Peru, the Sendero Luminoso (Shining Path), whose members were known as senderistas. The party was founded in the late 1960s by Abimael Guzmán who featured prominently in their propaganda. The Shining Path grew into a sizeable organisation under his leadership and began a guerrilla war after boycotting the 1980 elections. The conflict that followed was characterised by extreme brutality on both sides, with some of the government-trained anti-communist militias, such as the Grupo Colina, operating as death squads. By the early 90s, the Shining Path controlled much of south and central Peru. However, the conflict became more difficult for them with the emergence of the Túpac Amaru Revolutionary Movement, alongside peasant self-defence groups. In 1992, Guzmán was captured, leading to the end of the conflict.

No one wil take your land away, sister this is our revolution! A poster designed by Jesús Ruiz Durand to promote the agrarian reforms of Juan Velasco Alvarado, c.1968–1970. Apart from that of Cuba, it was the largest reform programme of its kind in Latin America, assisted by a vast propaganda campaign, much of it produced by the Sistema Nacional de Apoyo a la Movilización Social (National System of Support for Social Mobilization, or SINAMOS). Founded specifically to create propaganda promoting the programme, SINAMOS printed tens of thousands of posters during the period of agrarian reform. Often designed by Jesús Ruiz Durand they featured bold slogans alongside graphic, pop art-style images of workers.

Every bullet – one German. A poster published by the Polish Home Army during the Warsaw Uprising of 1944, urging the efficient use of ammunition by the insurgents. The operation was instigated by the resistance (Home Army) to coincide with the German retreat and the advance of the Red Army. In addition to driving the occupiers out of the city, the Uprising was also intended to establish Polish authority before the Soviets could seize control. However, Stalin deliberately halted the Red Army outside the city, allowing the Germans to regroup and crush the resistance.

A government poster from the Bush War (1964–1979) urging civilians to look out for weapons. The 'terrorists' of the text are fighters in Robert Mugabe's Zimbabwe African National Union (ZANU) and Joshua Nkomo's Zimbabwe African People's Union. The conflict ended minority white rule in Rhodesia, which was renamed Zimbabwe Rhodesia. However, this new state was not internationally recognised and the war continued until an agreement was signed that free elections would be held. The subsequent election was won by Mugabe in 1980, who became the first Prime Minister of Zimbabwe.

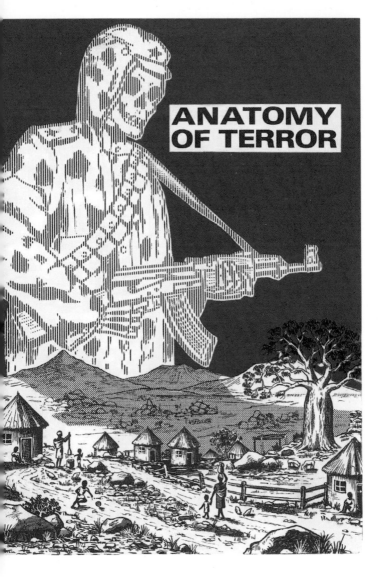

The cover of a booklet issued in 1974 by the Rhodesian Ministry of Information. It shows a skeletal communist guerrilla holding a Kalashnikov, looming over a small village settlement. The booklet was published during the Bush War (1964–1979), fought between the Rhodesian government and various guerrilla groups. It included graphic photographs, stating that they were evidence of the 'many atrocities perpetrated by the so-called Freedom Fighters of Rhodesia', and was intended for distribution abroad as an exposé of the rebels' alleged brutality.

A painting by Constantin Nitescu (1935–) titled *Omagiu* (Tribute), c.1980s. It shows Nicolae and Elena Ceauşescu greeting a crowd of children. Nicolae Ceauşescu (1918–1989) was General Secretary of the Romanian Communist Party from 1965 to 1989, with Elena serving as his deputy from 1980 to 1989. From the early- to mid-1970s, Romanian media and propaganda increasingly focused on building a cult of personality around Ceauşescu; his image was reproduced abundantly on posters, paintings, stamps, billboards and more. Romanian propaganda also grew more nationalistic, with a focus on the nation's historical struggles (and leaders) while concurrently downplaying the role of the Soviet Union in recent Romanian history. Despite this, by the late 1980s anti-government sentiment had led to the first signs of civil unrest. In December 1989, following riots across the country, Nicolae and Elena were captured, sentenced to death and executed by firing squad.

A poster of Slobodan Milošević inside a Yugoslavian bus, 1989. At this time, Milošević was growing in prominence at the head of the 'anti-bureaucratic revolution' that would ultimately deliver him the presidency of the Socialist Republic of Serbia, a position he held from 1997 to 2000. A key figure in the Yugoslav Wars, following his arrest in 2001, he was the first sitting head of state to be charged with war crimes. At his trial in the Hague he conducted his own defence, dying of a heart attack in his cell before the final verdict. He was found to be part of a criminal enterprise that used ethnic cleansing to remove Croats, Bosniaks and Albanians from areas in Croatia, Bosnia and Herzegovina, and Kosovo. Although not directly guilty of genocide, he had broken the Genocide Convention by failing to prevent it or hold those responsible to account.

This postcard design pokes fun at the US, after the Yugoslav Army shot down an F-117A Nighthawk using a Yugoslav version of a Soviet-era surface-to-air missile. The Nighthawk was the first operational aircraft to employ stealth technology, using a faceted design and cooled exhaust system to minimise detection. The 'invisible' plane was shot down on 27 March 1999, during the Kosovo War, near the town of Buđanovic (these details are reproduced on the postcard's faux stamp). The pilot safely ejected and was later recovered during a search and rescue mission. The downing was a triumph for the government and subsequently featured in dozens of propaganda designs, both physical and digital (Serbia ran a small but effective online psychological warfare campaign during the conflict).

Smrt okupatorjem in izdajalcem!

Death to the occupiers and traitors! A partisan poster from the Second World War (1944) showing Nazi and traitorous ghouls marching ahead of a broad trail of blood, at the far end of which is a massive, defiant Partisan fist. The Slovene Partisans formed part of the broader Yugoslav partisan movement and were among the most effective anti-Nazi resistance groups in Europe. Nikolaj Pirnat, the artist who designed this poster, was interned in Gonars concentration camp in Italy. When Italy switched sides to join the Allies in October 1943, Pirnat began producing propaganda for the partisans.

Slovene Partisan poster from the Second World War (1944). The Slovene
Partisans formed part of the broader Yugoslav partisan movement and were
among the most effective anti-Nazi resistance groups in Europe. This poster's
artist, Nikolaj Pirnat, was interned in Gonars concentration camp in Italy
before joining the partisans as a propagandist in 1943 and producing much
of the movement's instantly recognisable art.

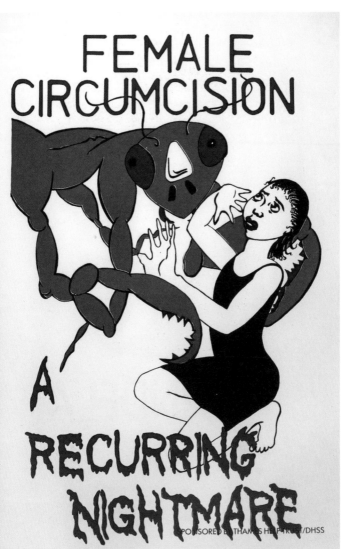

FEMALE CIRCUMCISION

A RECURRING NIGHTMARE

FOR INFORMATION TO: FORWARD, AFRICA CENTRE, 38 KING ST, COVENT GARDEN, LONDON WC2. TEL: 379 6889

SPONSORED BY THAMES HELP TRUST/DHSS

Anti-female genital mutilation poster from 1980, produced and published in the UK by the Africa Centre for distribution in Somalia. For reasons of inequality, involving traditional sexual control, Somalia has one of the highest rates of female genital mutilation.

A poster in support of the campaign to free Nelson Mandela (1918–2013), the prominent anti-apartheid activist who was imprisoned for 27 years after being arrested in 1962 for conspiring to overthrow the state. Launched by Oliver Tambo and the African National Congress, from exile in London, the Free Nelson Mandela campaign became a global cause during the 1980s. Popular music played a central part in bringing attention to his plight. In 1984, the Special A.K.A. single 'Free Nelson Mandela' reached number 9 in the UK chart. Mass concerts were organised, such as the Freedom Festival at Clapham Common in London (1986) and the Nelson Mandela 70th Birthday Tribute (1988). He was finally released by State President F. W. de Klerk in 1990 and went on to serve as the first President of South Africa between 1994 and 1999.

(S)hell

normaal   super

IN ZUIDELIJK AFRIKA

UITGAVE: KOMITEE ZUIDELIJK AFRIKA, DA COSTASTRAAT 88, AMSTERDAM.
WERKGROEP KAIROS, CORNELIS HOUTMANSTRAAT 17, UTRECHT.

A Dutch anti-apartheid poster from 1978, criticising Shell's involvement in apartheid South Africa after other prominent oil companies, such as Mobil and Texaco, had pulled out. Designed by Jan Koperdraat, the poster shows two petrol pumps: the left one reads 'normal' and shows a black man behind bars, while the right one reads 'super' and shows a tank at the scene of a massacre. The poster was one of a series issued jointly by the Komitee Zuidelijk Afrika (Southern Africa Committee, KZA) and Werkgroep Kairos, as part of a campaign directed primarily against Shell. Although global in its scope, the movement was mostly active in Britain, the Netherlands and the US. Despite the immense publicity the campaign achieved, Shell maintained operations in South Africa.

Above: **Kim Il-Sung is truly loyal to Russia and is the servant who serves me best**. A leaflet from the Korean War (1950–1953) showing Kim Il-Sung (Supreme Leader of North Korea from 1948 to 1994) as Stalin's puppet.

Right: **Sons or daughters, let's have two children and raise them well**. A population planning campaign poster from 1974. The objective of this drive was to stabilise population growth, with the promise that 'small and prosperous families' would deliver increased living standards. Fertility rates had been high in the 1950s, but began declining rapidly in the 1970s. South Korea had implemented its first population planning policies in the 1960s.

1981
1,000불
국민소득의
길

딸·아들 구별 말고
둘만 낳아 잘 기르자

1974 년은 세계 인구의 해   보건사회부 · 대한가족계획협회

Around the time of this campaign the government had set itself the aim of achieving a two-child replacement fertility rate by 1981. This is demonstrated in the poster by a brother and sister, skipping into a prosperous future. The text at the top of the arrow reads: 'the road to $1,000 personal income by 1981.' The campaign also touched on the issue of selective abortion, where the preference for sons prompted many families to abort female foetuses. The drive against selective abortion was followed by several similar operations that were ultimately successful, but the population policies ended up being 'too successful' insofar as they led to a huge decline in fertility rates as well as an ageing and, as of recently, declining population.

1808, 1936, once again for our independence. A poster from the Spanish Civil War showing a soldier's hands reloading a rifle against a backdrop of Republican colours. The date on the poster is a reference to the Peninsular War fought over a century earlier against the occupying French. That war began in Madrid in 1808, with the Dos de Mayo uprising against French troops who were occupying Spain as part of Napoleon's Iberian campaign. The uprising marked the beginning of a six-year war with France that quickly developed into a battle for national independence. This poster was designed by the prominent propagandist Josep Renau. During the Civil War he was appointed Director General for Fine Arts, a position that allowed him to recruit Picasso to the Republican cause. This catalyst would eventually yield one of the latter's best-known works, the anti-war painting *Guernica* (1937).

All militias merged in the Popular Army. This Republican poster from the Spanish Civil War (1937) shows a soldier's head in profile, covered in the flags of various organisations and nations. These are (clockwise from top left): the Confederación Nacional del Trabajo (a group of anarcho-syndicalist labour unions), the Basque Country, the Second Spanish Republic, Catalonia and Valencia, the Popular Front, Andalusia, Madrid, and the Communists. The poster was designed by Emeterio Melendreras for the Sindicato de Profesionales de las Bellas Artes, a propaganda art collective formed in Spain at the start of the war by the Unión General de Trabajadores (see also p152). It was published in Madrid by the city's defence council, the Junta Delegada de Defensa.

Read anarchist books and you will be a man. A Civil War poster encouraging citizens to read anarchist literature. It was published by the Sociedad General de Publicaciones in Barcelona along with another by the same artist depicting the outline of a soldier alongside the text: 'Anarchist books are weapons against fascism.'

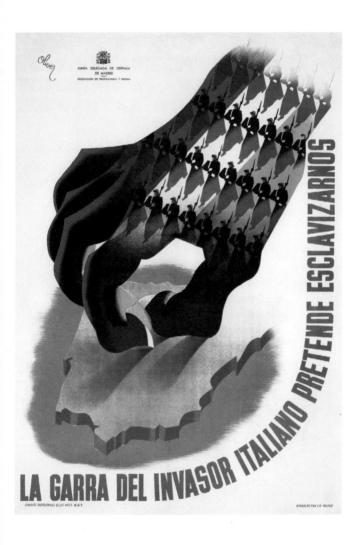

The claw of the Italian invader intends to enslave us. A Republican poster from the Spanish Civil War (1936) showing the claw of Italy reaching into Spain. It was published at the start of fascist Italy's intervention in the Civil War on the Nationalist side, an action which would ultimately see some 80,000 Italian soldiers committed to the conflict. The poster was one of a number issued during the war by the Madrid Defence Council condemning both Italian and German support for the Nationalists. Designed by Amado Mauprivez Oliver for the propaganda art collective Sindicato de Profesionales de las Bellas Artes.

The exported orange is the food of the people and the weapon to fight the foreign invader. This poster from the Spanish Civil War (1938) shows an orange tree strangling a Nazi. It was designed by Luis Dubón Portales and issued by the Citrus Export Council (CEA). The CEA issued a number of similar posters during the war stressing the importance of fruit exports to assist the Republicans' war effort.

COMO HA SEMBRADO LA IGLESIA
SU RELIGION EN ESPAÑA

How the church sowed its religion in Spain. An anti-religious poster published by the Unión General de Trabajadores (UGT, General Union of Workers) during the Spanish Civil War (1936–1939). The Catholic Church was linked to the fascist Nationalists, supporting them from the outset. The war was viewed as a battle between the democratic Republicans and the fascist Nationalists, but also between godless communism (Republicans) and civilised Christianity (the Nationalists).

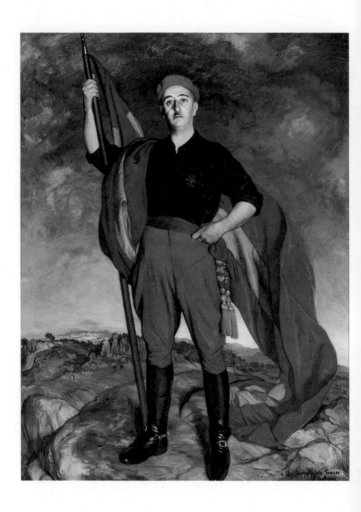

A portrait of Francisco Franco (1892–1975, dictator of Spain from 1939 until his death) painted by Ignacio Zuloaga in 1940. He wears the uniform of the Falange Española, a movement founded in 1933 by José Antonio Primo de Rivera, inspired by Italian fascism. The Falange naturally sided with the Nationalists during the Civil War, and in 1937 merged with other nationalist and anti-communist groups to form the 'Falange Española Tradicionalista y de las Juntas de Ofensiva Nacional Sindicalista' (Traditionalist Spanish Phalanx of the Councils of the National Syndicalist Offensive) under Franco's leadership. Zuloaga (1870–1945) was a Spanish painter and committed Nationalist during the Civil War, becoming acquainted with Franco in 1937 after writing an article in defence of their cause.

Franco keeps Spain's peace. A 1944 poster showing an armed knight blowing a horn alongside Death on horseback bristling with guns and bayonets, all flying over a ravaged Europe. Spain stands out as a beacon of peace among the carnage. Under Franco, Spain was officially neutral during the Second World War. With the exception of the División Azul (Blue Division), a volunteer unit which fought with the Germans on the Eastern Front, Franco largely refused to involve Spain in the war.

DET GÄLLER OSS

gå in i Frivilligkåren

It is our cause – join the Volunteer Corps. This 1939 poster shows a man protecting a child from an advancing tank. It was published for the Svenska Frivilligkåren (Swedish Volunteer Corps), a force of 10,000 men who had volunteered to help Finland fight the Soviet Red Army during the Winter War (1939–1940). The Corps also included a few hundred Norwegians and Danes. With the signing of the Moscow Peace Treaty in 1940, Finland ceded nine per cent of its territory to the USSR. The poor performance of the Red Army in this theatre encouraged Hitler to launch Operation Barbarossa against the Soviets in 1941.

Nuclear protection initiative for our future. On June 13/14 1981, YES. A poster showing a woman walking children past a nuclear cooling tower. Designed by Pierre Brauchli and published in 1981, the poster promotes a vote (or popular initiative) held in the canton of Bern against the construction of nuclear facilities. It was one of several designed by Brauchli protesting nuclear energy. The design borrows from Albrecht Anker's 1872 painting *The School Walk*.

สตรี สังคม สุรา

• มักพา **ความลับ** รั่ว •

Women, socialising and liquor often lead to secrets slipping. This anti-gossip poster from the 1960s shows a military officer leaking secrets while out partying. It was issued by the Armed Forces Security Centre, whose emblem is printed on the bottom right, below the drinks. The poster was one of a number conveying an anti-gossip message. Another in the series shows a similar scene, with a drunken officer leaking secrets to a seductive spy.

Turkish anti-communist cartoon published in 1949 in *Aydede* magazine. The illustration shows a giant hand labelled 'national unity' trimming a communist's hammer and sickle with a pair of scissors in such a way that only a star and crescent remain, causing the communist to fall. *Aydede* magazine was founded in 1922 and was relatively short-lived, being published from January until November that year, when the magazine's founder and editor, Refik Halit Karay (1888–1965), was forced into exile. Karay returned to Turkey in 1938, resuming the publication of *Aydede* in 1948, before eventually closing it down permanently in 1949.

Italya — Afrikaya medeniyet götürüyorum

I'm bringing civilisation to Africa. The front cover of *Akbaba* magazine showing a colossal Italian soldier loaded with armaments, wearing a gas mask and distinctive Bersaglieri hat, charging into Ethiopia equipped with numerous armaments, while an Ethiopian man looks up at him in horror. This issue was published during the Second Italo-Ethiopian War (1935–37), when fascist Italy invaded and annexed Ethiopia as part of Mussolini's aggressive expansionist policy. This action drew condemnation from around the world, with *Akbaba* emerging as one of the most vehement and consistent critics. Founded in 1922 as a satirical weekly, the magazine gained a reputation for its pointed attacks on world figures. Throughout the Second World War it targeted all the key players. However, during the Cold War it shifted focus, satirising those involved in conflicts closer to home, including Syria and Cyprus. It finally closed in 1977.

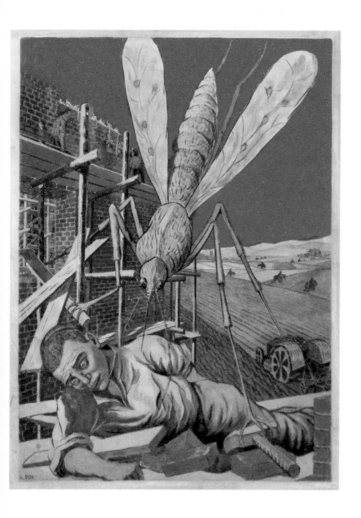

A Soviet-era anti-malaria poster by A. Volkov, from 1930. After instigating a malaria control programme in the 1920s, the Soviets went on to develop a more methodical approach in their efforts against the disease in the 1930s. Between 1937 and 1941, using a combination of DDT, mosquito nets and antimalarial medicines, the incidence of malaria declined by 47 per cent.

COMBAT READINESS

CONDOM READINESS

Produced by Public Health, NRA
Sponsored by USAID

An anti-AIDS poster published in c.1995 by the Ugandan Ministry of Health showing a soldier daydreaming about a girl. The poster was published during the government's huge AIDS awareness and prevention campaign – officially the National AIDS Control Program – which was launched in 1986 with the help of the UN and WHO. The campaign would last until 1995 and result in a massive decline in AIDS transmission. The 'NRA' on the soldier's helmet refers to the National Resistance Army, which would evolve into today's Uganda People's Defence Force.

DO NOT SHOOT EACH OTHER SHOOT AIDS.

PUBLISHED BY STD/AIDS CONTROL PROGRAMME, MINISTRY OF HEALTH, P.O.BOX 8, ENTEBBE UGANDA).

Ugandan anti-AIDS poster published in 1996 by the Ministry of Health showing a soldier firing condoms into the air. This poster was part of the country's long-running National AIDS Control Program. During the campaign, the government issued millions of often eccentric posters like this one, urging safe sex, symptom awareness and monogamy.

In one's own house, one's own truth, one's own might and freedom. A postcard showing the Ukrainian flag and loosely quoting Taras Shevchenko's poem, 'To my fellow-countrymen, in Ukraine and not in Ukraine, living, dead and as yet unborn, my friendly epistle'. The design, also printed on posters, was one of many produced by Ukrainian nationalists during their struggle for statehood following the First World War.

З Новим Роком!

A New Year's card from the 1950s, designed by Ukrainian artist Volodymyr Kaplun. It depicts an angelic knight holding the Ukrainian flag, standing victorious over a Soviet monster with a ruined building in the background, the sign above its door reading 'USSR'. During the Second World War Kaplun served in the Ukrainian National Army, a short-lived military force formed in 1945 from the remnants of Ukrainian divisions that had fought with the Germans against the Soviets. After the war, Kaplun was interned by the Allies in Italy, before emigrating to Argentina upon his release in 1948.

An anti-Soviet poster published in America, showing the Soviet bear devouring Ukraine. It was produced for a demonstration organised by the 'National Committee to Protest the Russification of Ukraine' held in Washington DC on 16 September 1984. The rally attracted some 10,000 participants who marched on the Soviet embassy.

This anti-segregation poster from the 1960s was produced by the Episcopal Society for Cultural and Racial Unity (ESCRU). It shows black and white Christians on either side of a barbed wire fence, marked 'Segregation' and 'Separation', with the crucified Christ spanning the divide between the two. ESCRU was established in December 1959 to 'remove all vestiges of segregation from the life of the Church', and to campaign against segregation more broadly. The image was copied from an anti-apartheid poster distributed by Anglicans in Johannesburg, South Africa, during Holy Week in 1959.

Above: This anti-Nazi postcard from 1934 shows Hitler trying to intimidate Einstein. The image titled 'The Ignominy of the Twentieth Century' was designed by Italian-American artist Michael Califano and the card was sold to raise funds for Jewish refugees. A quote from Einstein also appeared on the reverse: 'Neither hatred nor persecution can stay the progress of science and civilization.'

Right: A poster from the Second World War dated 1942, showing a colossal book looming over a book-burning spree. The quote on its cover is from President Roosevelt. The phrase 'books are weapons in the war of ideas' was coined and adopted as a motto by the Council on Books in Wartime, an association of booksellers, publishers, librarians and other organisations founded in 1942. Roosevelt was one of the association's enthusiastic supporters, and the quote comes from a speech he delivered at a banquet held by the American Booksellers Association, one of the more prominent organisations within the Council. From 10 May 1933, book burnings were carried out in Germany and Austria by Nazi-dominated student groups, targeting books they deemed 'un-German', such as those written by Jewish, communist, socialist and liberal authors. The evil nature of the book burnings became a prominent theme in a series of posters, usually with an emphasis on the Council's motto.

This preparatory poster image from the Second World War (1943) shows determined soldiers from the USA, USSR, UK and China marching in step. Behind them are the flags of other Allied nations, including Greece, Norway, France and Brazil. Commissioned by the Office of War Information, the poster was never actually issued. The illustration is by Frank Robbins (1917–1994), a painter, comic book artist and writer, who worked for both DC and Marvel comics on characters such as Superboy, Batman, Captain America and the Man from Atlantis.

Another poster illustration from the Second World War (1943) showing Allied guns firing in unison. Designed by Austrian-American artist Henry Koerner (1915–1991), this was an early conceptual design for the famous 'United we are strong, United we will win' poster issued by the Office of War Information (OWI) later in the year. The flags depicted in the final design are those of Brazil, Belgium, Norway, Britain, Mexico, China, the Soviet Union, Australia and Czechoslovakia (the last in place of the flag of Greece shown in this picture). Koerner had emigrated from Austria in 1938 following its annexation by Germany, working for the OWI and later the graphic division of the Office of Strategic Services. He designed a number of the war's more well-known posters, including *Someone Talked* (1942) and *Save Waste Fats* (1943). Before being discharged from the army, he was assigned to produce court sketches of the defendants at the Nuremberg trials. After the war he was best known for his paintings in the Magical Realist style and his numerous covers for *Time* magazine.

Pvt. Joe Louis says_

"We're going to do our part
... and we'll win because
we're on God's side"

For additional copies write to Graphics Division, Office of Facts and Figures, Washington, D. C. . . . Specify GPO Jacket No. 460989.
☆ U.S. GOVERNMENT PRINTING OFFICE : 1942—O

A Second World War (1942) poster featuring 'the Brown Bomber', boxer Joe
Louis (1914–1981). Arguably the greatest boxer of all time, he was world
heavyweight champion from 1937 to 1949. In 1935 Louis suffered his first
professional loss, being knocked out by the German, Max Schmeling. The
defeat was used by the Nazis as proof of Aryan supremacy. The 1938 rematch,
one of the most important bouts in boxing history, lasted two minutes and
four seconds, after Schmeling was knocked out by a barrage of punches
from Louis. A pivotal moment in sports history, it was the first time many
white Americans had supported a black sportsman. Louis served in a racially
segregated regiment during the war. When questioned on the subject he
said, 'Lots of things wrong with America, but Hitler ain't going to fix them.'

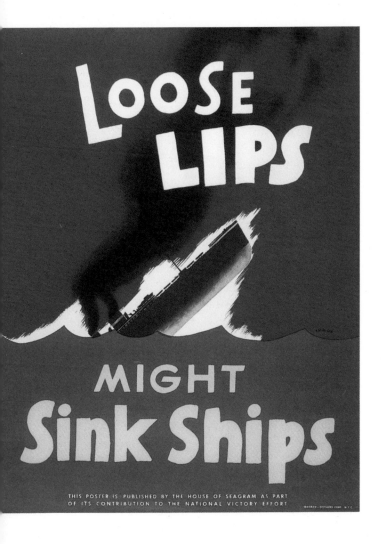

This famous poster was part of a general campaign of American propaganda during the Second World War, advising servicemen and other citizens to avoid careless talk concerning secure information that might be of use to the enemy. The poster was designed by Seymour Rinaldo Goff (1904–1992), director of the art department at Seagram distillers. Seagram used their connections to distribute them (along with postcards with the same image) to bars, restaurants and government facilities.

A poster from the Second World War (1942) showing three American children playing on a lawn onto which is cast the shadow of a huge, ominous swastika. The eldest boy holds a toy US Air Force plane, while the youngest carries a United States flag, and the girl has a doll that, having been touched by the shadow, lies lifeless. The poster was designed by Lawrence Beall Smith and published by the US Treasury.

Soldier Take Warning (1942). This painting by Salvador Dalí (1904–1989) depicts an American soldier looking at two prostitutes whose joint shape, along with the round glow from the lamp above them, resembles that of a skull. The US Office of War Information (OWI) was in the middle of an anti-venereal disease poster campaign and an initial design by Dalí was passed to the artist Bernard Perlin, an employee and prominent artist of OWI, who was supposed to prepare the work to be printed on posters, although it seems to have never been formally issued. Dalí lived in the US from 1940 until 1948, when he returned to Spain.

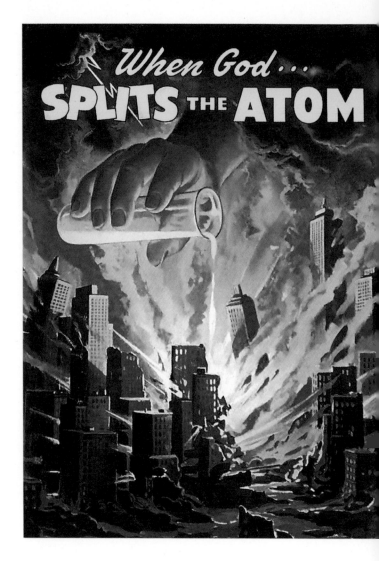

A Christian pamphlet published in 1946 prophesying imminent nuclear armageddon. The cover illustration shows the hand of God reaching from the clouds to pour destruction on a city from a test tube. The pamphlet (the full title of which is: *When God Splits the Atom: An Explanation of the Meaning of the Discovery and the Principles of Nuclear Fission in the Light of the Ancient Prophecies of the Bible*) was written by the prolific evangelical Adventist minister Carlyle B. Haynes (1882–1958), who argued that the Atomic Age and the expected attendant apocalypse had been foretold in biblical prophecies.

A button badge produced for the presidential campaigns of Richard Nixon (1913–1994) in the 1960s and 1970s. The slogan 'They can't lick our Dick' emerged in the early 1960s – unofficially at first – although it was used officially by the Nixon campaign on at least one occasion. An early mention of the button badge appears in a 1960 article published in *The Realist* magazine during Nixon's unsuccessful presidential campaign of that year: 'a novelty shop sells buttons that read :"They Can't Lick Our Dick".' Following a close battle with Vice President Hubert Humphrey, he won the 1968 election and was inaugarated in 1969. After being re-elected in 1972 his complicity in the Watergate scandal left him facing impeachment charges and potential removal from office, a situation which led to his resignation in 1974.

The front cover of a 1969 issue of *The Black Panther* newspaper, showing the profile of a weeping black G.I. with a photomontage of lynchings and police brutality across his helmet. The photograph to the top right is of Huey Newton, founder of the Black Panthers. The cover was designed by Emory Douglas, chief graphic designer and Minister of Culture for the Black Panther Party. Established in 1967 and distributed nationwide, *The Black Panther* was the party's official publication, raising its profile while keeping its readers updated on its activities and objectives.

A Black Panther poster from 1970, also designed by Emory Douglas (see left). With the use of simplified, often cartoon-like imagery, he sought to communicate sometimes complex political issues in a comprehensive fashion, stating: 'After a while it flashed on me that you have to draw in a way that even a child can understand to reach your broadest audience without losing the substance or insight of what is represented.'

A 1983 poster designed by Terry Forman for the Fireworks Graphics Collective in San Francisco. During the 1970s and 1980s Grand Juries were held and subpoenas subsequently issued against Puerto Rican, Black and Mexican independence organisations. Under US law, anyone refusing to co-operate with a Grand Jury can be imprisoned for up to two years. The Federal Bureau of Investigation exploited this system as a means of gathering information about these groups and their members, as well as jailing activists.

This poster, c.1984, also designed by Terry Forman for the Fireworks Graphics Collective, advertised a demonstration against a Ku Klux Klan (KKK) march in San Francisco. In the 1980s the KKK (and other white supremacist organisations) were on a recruitment drive across America. The counter-rally was successful, the police being forced to escort Klan members out of the area for their own protection.

"Careful, honey, he's anti-choice."

This pro-choice (in support of legal abortion) poster from 1981 shows two women quietly discussing an 'anti-choice' man downstairs. The design was first published by Heresies, a New York-based feminist art collective founded in 1979. It originally featured in a 1981 issue of the group's magazine *Heresies: A Feminist Publication on Art and Politics* and was quickly reproduced on posters, leaflets, adverts and T-shirts by feminist organisations both in America and internationally.

„Самодержавіе.”

'Autocracy.' This postcard (c.1915) shows Grigori Rasputin (1869–1916) caressing Alexandra Feodorovna (1872–1918), the last Empress of Russia. The postcard was widely printed in Russia during the peak of Rasputin's notoriety, when rumours were circulating of an affair between the supposed mystic and Alexandra. It is widely held that Rasputin maintained a controlling influence over Alexandra. The caption on the card is something of a pun, reading *samoderzhaviye* (autocracy), while playing on the root word *derzhit* (to hold). His sinister reputation was deemed a threat to the Russian Empire, and he was assassinated by a group of noblemen in 1916. Alexandra Feodorovna was murdered (along with the rest of the Russian Imperial Romanov family) by Bolsheviks in 1918.

Above: A portrait of Stalin mounted on a tractor in Uzbek Soviet Socialist Republic, c.1940. The photograph was taken by Max Penson, a photojournalist who spent some three decades living in Tashkent documenting life in the new Soviet republic for the newspaper *Pravda Vostoka* (*Truth of the East*).

Right: Students at the Academy of Arts in Leningrad paint a massive portrait of Stalin ahead of May Day celebrations, 1934. During the Soviet era, 1 May (International Workers' Day) was celebrated with huge parades intended to display military prowess and technological achievements, orchestrated to demonstrate the progress of the USSR to the rest of the world.

ИНДИЙЦЫ И РУССКИЕ-БРАТЬЯ !
हिन्दी रूसी भाई-भाई !

Indians and Russians are brothers! This poster from 1956 shows a Russian and an Indian holding hands in front of their respective flags, with the caption in Russian and Hindi. Designed by Stanislav Zabaluev, the poster was published a year after Jawaharlal Nehru and Nikita Khrushchev visited each other's countries.

Жизнь победит!

Life will win! A poster (c.1971) showing a Vietnamese child reading a book on the wing of a downed American aircraft. It was designed by Viktor Koretsky (1909–1998), one of the Soviet Union's most famous propagandists and graphic designers. Influenced by the work of the German political photomontage artist John Heartfield (1891–1968) and Latvian Constructivist photographer Gustav Klutsis, he developed his own method of combining photography and traditional materials into impactful propaganda posters. He was awarded the Stalin prize for his work in 1946 and again in 1949.

Above: **I would learn Russian just because Lenin spoke it**. A poster from 1963, showing an African man smiling in front of a picture of shelves of books all bearing the single word Lenin on their spines. Designed by Vladimir Sachkov, the poster quotes a verse from Vladimir Mayakovsy's poem 'To Our Youth' (1927):
Even if I
were an elderly negro
and then
without being despondent or lazy
I would learn Russian
only because it
was spoken by Lenin

Right: **Wasps' nest**. A cartoon from 1981, showing wasp-fighters emerging from the nest marked **Pakistan**, carrying briefcases crammed with weapons, labelled with their respective destinations: **Iran, Afghanistan** and **India**. The text at the top reads: **In the territory of Pakistan there are centres of subversion working against Afghanistan, India and Iran**. The cartoon was drawn by Boris Starchikov and published in *Krokodil* (Crocodile) magazine – a source of much anti-Pakistan content throughout the 1980s. This content generally accused the country of sponsoring mujahideen fighters in Afghanistan (and elsewhere), where the USSR were fighting the Afghan-Soviet War (1979–1989). America and its Central Intelligence Agency also made regular appearances in these cartoons as paymasters of these various groups.

Цена номера 20 коп. Индекс 70448

На территории Пакистана имеются центры по проведению подрывной работы против Афганистана, Индии и Ирана.

ОСИНОЕ ГНЕЗДО

Рисунок Б. СТАРЧИКОВА

ЛЕНИН ВЕЛИКИЙ НАМ ПУТЬ ОЗА

Above: **The great Lenin illuminated our path**. A 1969 poster by Vasily Boldyrev. Slavery and racism were used by the Soviet Union as telling symbols of the imperialist West's corrupt, capitalist society. However, the depiction of black protagonists for this theme often relied on stereotypes contrary to the intended message.

Right: **No to racism!** A 1972 poster designed by Veniamin Briskin (1906–1982), showing workers attacking a member of the Ku Klux Klan.

A painting from 1976 by Dorzhiev Lubsan, who was later appointed People's Artist of the Buryat Autonomous Soviet Socialist Republic. It celebrates the Apollo–Soyuz mission of 1975, when the US Apollo module docked with the

Soviet Soyuz capsule and astronauts from both countries spent two days together in orbit. General Stafford, leader of the US crew, told his Soviet counterparts, 'I'm sure we have opened up a new era in the history of man.'

Above: **I'm happy to be breathing the same air as you!** An environmental poster (c.1980s) showing a couple sitting on a bench wearing gas masks, while factory chimneys pump out clouds of industrial pollution. The poster was one of a series of environmentalist prints issued by 'Fighting Pencil', a prominent graphic collective active during both the Second World War and the Cold War.

Right: **Diplomacy the American way**. A Soviet poster from 1986 showing a US 'diplomat' – his front half smartly business suited, while his back half is clad in military gear. American President Ronald Reagan (1911–2004) had met with the leader of the Soviet Union, Mikhail Gorbachev (1931–2022) at the Geneva Summit in 1985 and again at the Reykjavik Summit in 1986. Gorbachev wanted to ban all ballistic missiles, while Reagan was intent on continuing with his Strategic Defense Initiative (nicknamed the Star Wars programme). Despite these talks ending in failure, a new dialogue between the two countries had begun. The consequences of this new-found rapport included the 1987 Intermediate Nuclear Forces Treaty and, ultimately, the end of the Cold War.

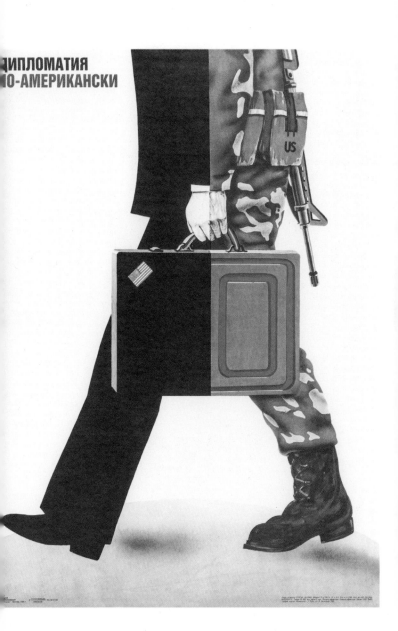

ДИПЛОМАТИЯ
ПО-АМЕРИКАНСКИ

Myth and reality. A 1984 poster designed by V. Slepukhin, showing the United States as a shark-like submarine, with missiles for teeth, posing as a harmless paper boat.

**НЕБО РОДИНЫ
ЗАЩИЩЕНО НАДЕЖНО!**

The sky of the motherland is safely protected! This poster from 1984 was designed by Vladimir Feklyaev (1947–) as part of a series celebrating the Soviet Armed Forces. It was published in Moscow by *Plakat* (literally 'Poster'), the official publishing house of the Central Committee of the Communist Party of the Soviet Union. The 'CA' (SA) on the soldier's epaulette stands for 'Soviet Army'.

A man carrying a child walks past a mural in Caracas, Venezuela, 2002. The figures are (left to right) Che Guevara, Saddam Hussein, Hugo Chávez, Fidel Castro and Muammar Gaddafi. In April 2002 Chávez, the Venezuelan

President, was ousted from power in a coup and arrested following a shootout near his offical residence. Popular support and the backing of loyal sections of the military led to him being restored to office within 24 hours.

Above: **30 years**. A detail from a poster produced at the end of the Vietnam War (1975) showing a gigantic fist punching a US B-52 in half.

Right: **Nixon must pay for our blood with his blood!** One of the most famous and reproduced designs of the Vietnam War, this poster, c.1972, shows a woman with a limp child in her arms, next to a bombed-out hospital. She reaches out to strike at a bomb bearing the face of Richard Nixon. It was likely published during, or in the wake of, Operation Linebacker II – an intense B-52 bombing campaign that sought to destroy major targets in the north. By this time, the US had adopted a strategy of intensive bombing in North Vietnam in an effort to speed the end of the conflict.

NIXON
PHẢI
TRẢ
NỢ
MÁU!

BỆNH VIỆN

RA SỨC RÈN LUYỆN QUÂN SỰ
SẴN SÀNG BẢO VỆ TỔ QUỐC

Above: **Saigon River commandos**. A North Vietnamese poster, c.1975, showing a Saigon River raid. This poster depicts the so-called *đặc công*, the special forces unit of the People's Army of Vietnam (PAVN), whose duties included commando raids and sabotage. They were known to US troops as sappers – a term drawn from the French *saper* (to undermine, to bring down), a vestige from their colonial period in the country. Following the Tet Offensive of 1968, these fighters became an especially prominent force within the PAVN and Viet Cong (the communist forces of South Vietnam, Laos and Cambodia). Small sapper units would penetrate US positions and bases, getting close enough to prevent the Americans' use of artillery or air strikes, and wreak havoc. Later in the war they would be an essential element in the PAVN and VC's 'blooming lotus' strategy, in which a small force would infiltrate an enemy position and then fight outwards.

Left: **Strive to train soldiers to be in a position to defend the nation!** A North Vietnamese poster from 1971.

Workers take a break next to a portrait of Josip Tito in the Crvena Zastava (Red Flag) car factory in Kragujevac (then the Socialist Republic of Serbia) sometime in the 1980s. The car on the production line is the Yugo 45. Based on the Fiat 127, the Yugo was marketed across Europe and America in the 1980s, until manufacture was halted by the Yugoslav wars (1991–2001). The Zastava factory itself was hit by NATO bombs in 1999. Thanks to its basic functionality and low cost, the Yugo has endured. Still common in countries of the region, it is a nostalgic symbol of the former Yugoslavia.

A portrait of Josip Tito by Boris Chaliapin, published in *Time*, October 1944. During his career Chaliapin illustrated over 400 covers for the magazine.

By 1944 Tito's partisans had begun to receive considerable aid from the Allies, especially Britain, and were able to ramp up their operations. Tito's partisans conquered Belgrade in October – when this portrait was published – and by 1945 controlled the majority of what would become Yugoslavia.

This election poster was published by the Zimbabwe African National Union–Patriotic Front (ZANU–PF) ahead of the 1980 general election. The election was held in what was then Southern Rhodesia, to determine who would lead the newly independent Zimbabwe. The Rhodesian Bush War (1964–1979) – a conflict between the Rhodesian government, Robert Mugabe's ZANU–PF and Joshua Nkomo's Zimbabwe African People's Union (ZAPU) – had ended with the Lancaster House Agreement, which had been negotiated in London. It resolved that Southern Rhodesia be briefly returned to British rule while the Commonwealth supervised the 1980 general election. The ZANU–PF subsequently won, taking 63 per cent of the vote. Mugabe would rule Zimbabwe for the next four decades until he was ousted in a 2017 coup.

A poster showing a graphic image of two guerrilla fighters in Zimbabwe, c.1977. The poster was published during the fifteen-year long Rhodesian Bush War (see previous page). The design was reproduced around the world, by different groups and in different languages, in support of the guerrillas' struggle against Rhodesia's white, minority-led government.

ACKNOWLEDGEMENTS

p15 Shah Marai / Stringer / Getty Images
p20 Albert Hilscher / Austrian National Library
pp26–27 mccool / Alamy Stock Photo
p38 © Henri Cartier-Bresson / Magnum Photos
p58 © Jean-François Batellier (1978) jf-batellier.com
p61 Chronicle / Alamy Stock Photo
p81 Francois Lochon / Getty Images
p83 Carolyn Cole / Getty Images
p90 brandstaetter images / Getty Images
p104 Barry Iverson / Alamy Stock Photo
p103 Thomas Coex / Getty Images
p114 Keystone Press / Alamy Stock Photo
p119 courtesy CAIN Archive cain.ulster.ac.uk
p128 © Estate of Abram Games abramgames.com
p132 *Ya nadie te sacará*, from the series La Reforma Agraria (1968-1973) by
Jesús Ruiz Durand. Offset print on paper, 99.4 x 68.7 cm. From the collction
of: Malba, Museo de Arte Latinoamericano de Buenos Aires. Ph: Nicolás
Beraza. © Jesús Ruiz Durand
p143 © Jan Koperdraat facebook.com/jankoperdraat/
p173 Salvador Dalí / DACS 2024
pp176–177 © Emory Douglas / DACS 2024
pp178–179 Principal artist: Terry Forman © Fireworks Graphic Collective /
Terry Forman fireworksgraphics.org
p182 Album / Alamy Stock Photo
pp196–197 Jose Caruci / Stringer / Getty Images
p202 © Steve McCurry / Magnum Photos
p203 Marshal Tito by Boris Chaliapin. Watercolour, gouache and graphite
pencil on board. National Portrait Gallery, Smithsonian Institution; gift of
Mrs. Boris Chaliapin. © 2008 Estate of Helcia Chaliapin
p204 © The Poster Collective / Christine Halsall

Above: 'Chávez Eyes' on a billboard in Guarenas, Venezuela. The idea for the design came from José Miguel España, a member of the campaign team that successfully helped elect Hugo Chávez for a fourth term as President in 2012. Following his death from cancer in 2013, the emblem was adopted by the new President, Nicolás Maduro.

Front cover: Illustration by FUEL. An adaptation of the Hungarian poster 'Protect Yourself' by György Pál (c.1970, see p72).

Back cover: An adaptation of the Soviet poster 'Don't Gossip!' by Nina Vatolina (1941).

Published in 2024

FUEL Design & Publishing
33 Fournier Street
London E1 6QE

fuel-design.com
@fuelpublishing

Designed and edited by Murray & Sorrell FUEL
Image research and text by Bradley Davies
@propagandopolis
Copy edited by FUEL and Fergal Stapleton
Essay © Robert Peckham

Distribution by Thames & Hudson / D. A. P.
ISBN: 978-1-7398878-5-8
Printed in Malaysia